REIKI
FOR THE SOUL

By the same author:

Practical Reiki
Reiki for Common Ailments
Shamanka
Modrost Velka Matka

REIKI
FOR THE SOUL

10 DOORWAYS TO INNER PEACE

MARI HALL

Thorsons

Thorsons
An Imprint of HarperCollins*Publishers*
77–85 Fulham Palace Road
Hammersmith, London W6 8JB

The Thorsons website address is www.thorsons.com

Published by Thorsons 2000

3 5 7 9 10 8 6 4 2

© Mari Hall 2000

Mari Hall asserts the moral right to
be identified as the author of this work

A catalogue record for this book is available
from the British Library

ISBN 0 7225 3891 X

Printed and bound in Great Britain by
Scotprint, Haddington

To my parents Dean and Ginny, my daughter Stacey,
and my students who have taught me the art of living and loving
without my masks. And to you who share my story…

CONTENTS

霊
気

REIKI FOR THE SOUL
INTRODUCTION

S OME of the work that people do to come into personal harmony can involve working with reactionary patterns of personality. These appear like layers that can be removed, much like pealing an onion. As the layers of the personality are exposed it takes time to integrate what is now presented. Gradually, each aspect of the personality is revealed, layer by layer, until the centre or the soul self is reached and the light can be fully experienced.

In essence, the layers of the personality are like masks that we have created in order to survive, to receive love and to be accepted. These masks can also keep us from experiencing our own divinity, or better yet, remembering that divinity. That is why we search outside ourselves first for the truth that lies hidden within.

What holds the mask in place is our thoughts, emotions, and demands of how we must be. This moves us away from our Spiritual nature, and from our inner peace.

We do not need to experience the opposite polarity to come into harmony or go from one extreme to another. Rather, we can move softly and gently into the centre of who we are authentically and in this our soul is open to the source. It has become the doorway for the Spirit to move through us.

Everything depends upon the extent of the problem and how deeply rooted it is. Each person is an individual that is made complex by reaction. Reiki helps us move into harmony in our minds, bodies and emotions, thus working on the root cause of physical illness. When our emotions and mind are harmonized we have moved closer to our Spiritual nature.

The essence of Reiki is unconditional love. It is the Spirit of God that moves through us encouraging us to live. Spirit sources the soul; Reiki brings the Spirit of God to mankind and thus sources the being to come into complete harmony. It nourishes the soul.

It is my intention to share with you the various doorways that I have opened and explored. Perhaps in sharing my personal journey you may also see which doorways you have closed with your reactions, thus blocking the energy for the Spirit to work through you. Conceivably, this book will serve as a key to unlock the doors and bring you into closer relationship with your divine nature. All I have written for you in these pages has been helped to heal because of my relationship with Reiki. Reiki has indeed been a major key for the discovery of myself and the beauty of all life.

I invite you, the reader, to stop for a moment and close your eyes. Take a deep breath and imagine that you are standing in front of a door. Are you willing to explore what is behind the door and possibly the others you will find here as well?

Be careful – your life might be changed as a result.

How to Use this Book

The basic concept of the book is the various doors we are given the choice to walk through and explore. We will be looking at our relationship to work, to partnership, parents, children, old people, ourselves and to stages of development. It is my intention to give you something to think about and to encourage you to become aware of the doorways in yourself that may remain closed. Doorways that you have the choice to open again yourself. It will give opportunity to explore and choose. It is not a self-development book. It is a book to touch your soul and be sourced by Spirit. It can be read through or picked up and dipped into. Watch where the page opens – is it a new doorway or one you have explored before? I have also included spaces to write thoughts, much like a journal, so that it will involve your interaction with yourself. Each chapter is a door; you hold the key in your hand to open it. As we move through the book the doors change and get lighter in colour. When we move closer to the soul self, the final door is opened to reveal the light of the Spirit, and you will have come home to inner peace and harmony...

I have used the name of 'God' throughout the book. In my heart and mind, 'God' has many names. This word has been used to denote something so profoundly special. The energy of 'God' includes male and female energy, nature and the universe. It is the loving, creative energy that is in everything. It is in us and surrounds us. If this word bothers you, I would ask you to translate it into something that holds this meaning for you. It is not restricted by religion, rather it touches the centre of all.

Shall we begin the journey?

An Introduction to Reiki

Reiki is a method of transferring universal life-giving energy for the harmony of the body, mind and soul. It addresses both the cause and effect of illness. It is transferred by gently placing the hands on your own body or that of another person. No religious philosophy is necessary to do Reiki, although it is thought of as a spiritual system. People of varying philosophical views, ages and life circumstances can practise this loving art.

I have always thought of Reiki as being universal unconditional love. The experience in both receiving and giving the energy is one of deep relaxation and an inner peace. The heart is opened to receive and give love. We are returned to a state of compassionate grace, the more we use this energy for self-treatment and the treatment of others. It is safely used any time, any place and for anything. You cannot receive too much Reiki. It is 100 per cent safe, effective, and gentle – Reiki does not intrude upon the person. It is the perfect complement to allopathic medicine and all forms of natural healing.

Reiki is a very old system that was rediscovered in the late 19th century by a man named Mikao Usui. Usui was passionate about discovering how a person could be healed by touch, and it became his life-long quest. He studied the Tibetan sutras and found what he thought were aspects of the wisdom, but he could not find the key to unlock the door to reveal it. In a spiritual practice of meditation and fasting he had a deeply moving experience and an initiation on Mount Kurama. As a result of this process he discovered the way to transfer this energy and began his own individual journey helping others. The association he formed all those years ago in Japan is still active in the teaching and practice of the Usui system of healing. Only recently have we been able to find out more about Usui. The man who remained like a mystery for many of us has now had life breathed into him. We have heard that he was compassionate, loved life and was dedicated to helping people. Usui actually adopted his spiritual principles that are part of our system of Reiki from the emperor of Japan in the Meiji era.

Reiki has been passed down from master to student. In the early times there were no masters of Reiki. Usui was considered a *Sensi*, a beloved teacher, a wise man. However, Hawayo Takata, a student of Chujiro Hayashi who had studied with Usui, brought Reiki to the West after the Second World War. In her teaching, there is the addition of the title 'Master'. This was a Western way to denote that someone had come into the practice of Reiki, studied with the initiating Master for a defined period of time, developed him- or herself spiritually and was now able to act as a mentor to a student. It was a long, slow process.

It is most important to understand that we come into the practice of Reiki by an initiation process that is carried out personally by the Reiki Master. The beauty of this system is that the personal contact and sharing of wisdom are the first steps you take on your own personal journey, in much the same way as you held your mum or dad's hand when you were learning to walk. The Master is a support for you. Someone to stand beside you as you enter into your own relationship with the energy. Their depth of practice will be important, as it will provide the space for you to go deep in yours. If I want to train to swim in the Olympics I will choose a coach who has swum there as well. Why would I take someone who has just learned to swim?

Unfortunately, the title of Reiki Master has been somewhat diluted. The title is sometimes given for very little effort. The depth that was once present in Usui's time is not always found. So the process of finding a Master of Reiki who has devoted time and energy to their practice can be frustrating. The student must be willing to ask questions of the person teaching the system and to feel comfortable with them. It is helpful to have a treatment from the teacher beforehand to tell if they feel like the person to teach you. There are schools of Reiki that are dedicated to the passing on of knowledge with integrity and love.

The last few years have seen a fast increase in the forms of Reiki and the amount of people practising this art. People from all over the world are willing instruments of the energy of Reiki. I have been personally blessed to see Reiki seem to spread like a wild fire across Europe. When I began teaching in Europe I was the first Usui Reiki Master in the UK. There was Radiance technique that had been started by Barbara Ray, a master from Takata's lineage. Now it is virtually all over Britain. When I moved to the then Czechoslovakia, I was the first Reiki Master here and now I have personally initiated over 30,000 Czech and Slovakian people into Reiki.

It is with the deepest respect and humility that I bow my head to Usui, thanks to whose dedication to finding the answers we now have Reiki in the world. In 1998, the form and standards for the teaching and professional practice of Reiki that I wrote and that have been used by my organization were accepted for affiliation to the Institute for Complementary Medicine. I was made a member of the British Register of Complementary Practitioners and appointed as a special advisor to the ICM on Reiki. It is my hope that we will adopt worldwide standards for the teaching of Reiki that will allow the purity of the system to remain intact. I continue to search for the way to bridge all forms of Reiki so that we can return to its centre. In the centre are the beauty and the power of Reiki. In the centre are Usui and the infinite love we can experience.

If you have never heard of Reiki before or had a Reiki treatment, I encourage you to do this. The absolute feeling of peace and relaxation is so nourishing. For those of you who have had an experience of Reiki, I trust it was rewarding for you. I am pleased to be with you here. It is my hope that something you read will evoke memories of times of spiritual change and deepening that you may have experienced. We can stand in the centre together and be sourced by each other.

My Journey into the Practice of Reiki

I came to Reiki out of a need to find something that would help me in my own healing process. I was only concerned about my physical malady as I was experiencing partial paralysis on my left side. I had bouts of standing up in the morning only to fall down immediately. The doctors had diagnosed a congenital back problem and said there was a good possibility that by the age of 40 I would be completely paralysed and confined to a wheelchair. I was so frightened with this diagnosis that I did not discuss it with anyone. I contemplated ending my life. For years, I had been closed and very sceptical and I could not imagine that anyone would want to take care of me. I went to the Reiki class thinking I had signed up for something that would not work. It seemed too far-fetched to be real. I had no intention of ever working on anyone else. What I experienced as a result of my willingness to treat myself was nothing less than miraculous.

My whole life changed. My deep depression lifted. I was more willing to accept what life had brought to me. I took responsibility for myself. I saw beauty and love around me and experienced it inside me. I was living life. I felt whole. After a year I was completely healed of my problem. It seemed only natural to turn this precious gift outwards to others. The more I changed, the more I responded to others. I was no longer closed. The layers of defence that I had so carefully built up all this time were stripped away one by one as I continued to work on myself. The deepest healing for me was not physical; it was emotional and mental. I began to have hope and trust in life. Even when things happened that I would normally have reacted to by closing or condemning, I saw as a gift to help me wake up spiritually.

My life began to have a natural ebb and flow; I was swimming with life, not against it. I remember my dad saying when I was little that if there was a hard way to learn something I would sign up for it. I had always demanded to make a door where there was none, instead of looking for the one that was there.

My relationship with everything changed. Some of the friends I had before didn't seem to have anything in common with me. We had spent our time talking about our misery. Misery loves company. Now that I was seeing and experiencing life differently there seemed nothing to talk about. I was no longer interested in being in a corporate agreement about how terrible men were, or how the boss misunderstood us.

I began a search for what was working in my life, what I needed to let go of to support this newness in me. I also felt the need to go back to a religious philosophy. To search for a church that resonated with me. I became involved in the Unity Church. I had never been to a church before that uplifted the individual. There was meditation before service and we held hands. It certainly gave me a different perspective to base a spiritual practice on. It encouraged me to be free to express my faith if I wanted. I was not required to witness in any way. By being myself I was the witness to God's love, Reiki and humankind.

I began to see my part in the failed relationships I'd had; how I continued to bring into my life exactly what I needed to heal if I so chose. I had been very hurt as a child and stopped trusting anyone. At the age of three, I decided that I would no longer cry. It takes so much life energy to hold back the tears for so many years. So the emotions came up to be expressed and released. I did not need to understand why, only to do Reiki on myself. I allowed the natural process of coming back into my centre to continue.

I realized that I had held onto so much resentment in my life that it had continued to make me out of balance. I was righteously resentful. After all, look what had happened in my life. As I released this resentment I could also see things from a different perspective. I understood deeply that people reacted and that their reactions gave me the opportunity to react. Reaction was nothing more than fear driven and it is what kept us from living in the precious moment of now. I could see how the world was constructed of people who had forgotten their basic truth of oneness.

In this moment of deep understanding I chose to become a Reiki Master. I wanted to become a vehicle for others to come back into their own harmony so that together we could co-create peace in our world. War is an outward manifestation of an internal problem. If we were all peaceful there would be no need for war. We could embrace each other as brothers and sisters. This has been the reason for my work with Reiki, and the vision that I hold before me. I went to such an extreme in my quest to save the world I ended up on the other side of the stream and righteous about what that looked like and how people should be. Life had given me another opportunity to wake up. I listened and made some corrections in my approach to living once again.

Continuing the practice of Reiki and being open to life, I have returned to a centre point. I do not need to save the world. I can do my part by being clear and loving. I can and do facilitate change. The people always have choice. We can all create peace together. I am by no means done with living. In many ways I feel as if I have just started. I certainly have not arrived at the top of the mountain to proclaim 'I am wonderful – look at me'. I have felt in my soul that the way to harmony is not climbing above others but to go deep inside oneself and bring light to our own darkness. The way to be transformed is becoming one with yourself and in this moment you are also one with all others.

I have found that Reiki gives me the ability to process life events in a clearer, more objective way. By using Reiki on a daily basis to stay in harmony I am better able to handle life's messages. I know that all events in my life are miracles if I am open to receive them. It is life's way of waking me up and bringing me back into the centre where the love is. The more resistance I have, the more of my ego is involved. I use Reiki to release my need to be right and safe. It is a process that becomes part of your life like breathing. I am not separate from Reiki – I am Reiki and it supports me to live a life with much more majesty and grace.

The Concept of Change

As we explore new possibilities by stepping through doorways, we are brought face to face with change. On the surface we may say we are ready for change in our lives. Yet also with change comes fear. Our minds have invested so much in how we are at this very moment, so change brings an unknown equation. The mind does not know how the newly changed 'me' will be and will attempt to hold on to what is known, even if it no longer works in our lives and has ceased to nourish us. The entire world is in a state of change. There are stepping-stones to change. See what stepping-stone you may be standing on in regards to certain areas of your life.

THE FIRST STEPPING-STONE, PULLING APART

It is like unravelling a sweater when the yarn is pulled. In moments like this our lives seem to be unravelling. The puzzle that was so perfectly put together no longer looks right. We see where we have forced some of the pieces to fit into place. All our energy is involved in keeping the status quo and it simply becomes too much.

THE SECOND STEPPING-STONE, WANTING

Once we understand that life is asking us to change, it becomes important to decide just what it is we want and also what we are no longer wanting in our lives. When faced with this sorting out space, sometimes it is easier to figure out what we do not want, what has to go. From what is left over it is easier to choose what we want to keep and to bring to ourselves.

THE THIRD STEPPING-STONE, LETTING GO

To let go of the things we no longer want or need sometimes involves pain, especially if we have invested so much energy in being right. Righteousness can bring pain as we let go of the excess baggage in our lives. We must also lose being right.

THE FOURTH STEPPING-STONE, ADJUSTING

Once we have let go of something there is a time for us to integrate the change, to settle back into this new space so that we can begin to feel what we want, rather than need. Needing something to make us feel complete is the mind's fear of the unknown. Very often, if we are not careful, we will bring our needs into our lives in the form of needy people. If this occurs we are just constructing the same old puzzle again. We need to take the time to allow ourselves to feel what we really want.

THE FIFTH STEPPING-STONE, SURRENDER

We release all the endless questions and need to know and allow God to send to us what is truly important in this moment. We enjoy what life brings to us, rather than trying to make it like we think it should be. We are more able to see the gift in every moment and love accepting it.

THE SIXTH STEPPING-STONE, IN THE SWIM

We are in the flow of life rather than trying to swim upstream. We are supported where once it was a struggle. We have released our necessity to control. We are in fact 'out of control'. We enjoy the journey and take in all we experience. We are on our return back to the centre and to God.

The only time we experience pain is when we refuse to learn the lesson of that particular step or doorway in the journey. When we get fixed and know how things should have been we will either want to retreat to the last most comfortable place, or refuse to go forward. This is called resistance. Our resistance to change causes pain.

Where in your life are you feeling resistance in pain? Has life been supporting you to let go and let God in? I suggest that you take the time now to write down these feelings of resistance in the space below. As you read further in the book you may find you have the key to let go.

I find I am resistant in regards to:

_____

_____

_____

_____

THE DOORWAY OF
OURSELVES

WE are given many opportunities to come into a more loving relationship with ourselves. Every time we look in the mirror in the morning we have the choice to love or to see what needs to be fixed or made better before we love ourselves. I remember the first time I was told this. I thought how difficult is it to look into the mirror in the morning and say I love you. I made the decision that I would do this every morning for a month.

Good Morning, I Love You

I woke up the first morning, padded my way to the bathroom, and looked in the mirror. 'My goodness,' I thought. 'Look at my hair standing up on end – I certainly look terrible.' My face was all puffy and swollen. I began my normal critical look at the woman who stood before me. 'You need to lose weight and get more sleep. You need to take better care of yourself. What is wrong with you anyway?' All these and more judgements and accusations tumbled through my mind in rapid succession. I brushed my teeth and the toothpaste landed on my nightgown. 'Clumsy' was my judgement. I turned and stepped into the shower, and as the warm water ran over my body I looked down and saw that my legs needed to be shaved. 'You teach about transforming lives and you do not even take time for yourself – look at you.'

Again, I was brought face to face with myself as I blow-dried my hair and styled it. 'Well, that's better, but…' I avoided looking at my self except to dab on the make-up I felt would make me look more acceptable to others. I blotted my lipstick on a tissue and heard 'I'm OK now?' The voice seemed sad and far away. I looked into the mirror, this time at the woman who had taken so much abuse from me since awakening. 'Pardon, did you say something?' I asked out loud. The eyes of the woman welled up with tears. 'You said you would tell me you loved me every day for a month. I was looking forward to receiving this love and all you did was belittle me. I want you to love me. I need your love. Am I so unlovable?' Tears were spilling down her cheeks as she reminded me that I had broken my promise to her. Her face was washing away all the make-up that had been applied. Her eyes were red rimmed, her nose began running and my heart broke open with grief. I remembered saying those same words to my parents. 'Am I so unlovable?' I sat there for what seemed like hours talking to the woman in front of me. I told her I was sorry for not seeing her beauty. I asked her forgiveness and also talked about the cost of not loving her as I realized that by not letting self love in fully I also had less space to be filled by others' love.

The next morning, as I lay in my bed, I put my hands on myself, giving myself Reiki. I thought about the woman in the mirror and that most of the time I felt far removed from her. It was easy to criticize her. I wanted more for her. I wanted her to feel loved. There was a pressure that had been building up in my chest as I was thinking about all the times I had not loved her, had not loved myself. I responded to this pressure with my hands, giving myself Reiki. Finally, I thought it was time to get up and start my day. I walked into the bathroom and stood in front of the mirror and said, 'Good morning Mari, I love you.' The woman looked into my eyes and said, 'I love you too.'

Remember the times you have looked into the mirror in the morning. What were some of the things you said to yourself? Have you reached the state of harmony where loving yourself is easy, and if so, how did that happen? What can you say about yourself that is positive and reaffirming? If you had to reassure your child and that child were you, what would you need to hear?

_____

_____

_____

_____

We are also brought into relationship with ourselves through other people. We are given moments to see ourselves both at our best and worst. There is a mirror that others hold up for us to look into. Sometimes it is obvious that we are seeing ourselves; other times our first impulse is to deny that the person could be anything like us at all.

Where is She in You?

Have you ever been told you are just like your mother? Or that you are behaving just like your dad? When I was little my mom told me that I looked like my great grandmother Shuburgh. To me, that was not a compliment because in all the photos of her that I had seen, she was formidable. She reminded me of a general in the army. What I had not seen was the picture my mother carried around of her in her heart. This was the closest person to her in her family. The one who loved her undeniably. My mom was raised in a very Victorian home where children were seen and not heard. She could be all she was with her grandma Mary. When her grandmother passed away it was the little Ginny who, not being allowed to cry, put her silent tears into the coffin. But, when I was little, I could only see from my perspective. And I was hurt that she thought I was so ugly.

So many times we do not see all the facets of the jewel that life is presenting to us. We only see it through the filter of our reactions in life. One of the biggest things I have come to terms with in my adult life is to see my beauty. For so long, I had held on to the belief that I was the ugly duckling of the family, the one who did not fit in, and the third wheel on the bicycle. Fortunately, I do not have that opinion any more.

Here is another of my many mirrors…

It was my first meal in Sammy Ling, a Buddhist retreat centre in Scotland. I stood in the line with my bowl in my hand. A woman wild as could be streamed past me, knocking me as I stood. She came close to me and screamed obscenities into the room, breaking the spell of peace. She left and I lost my hunger.

Later, as I stood in the line at dinner, bowl in hand, she appeared again. She was witch-like, her hair all standing almost on end, and she was wizened, all craggy and bent. Again, she knocked me with her body. Almost shouting in my ear, she yelled obscenities into the room again. 'She is the one who taught sailors to cuss,' I thought. I placed my bowl down and walked from the room without eating, my expectations of a peaceful meal shattered like a glass thrown against the floor.

In the morning as I said my prayers for a day to bring me closer to my divinity, I could hear the people going downstairs for breakfast so I followed the crowd and ended up in the dinning room once again.

'Today will be different, I am different,' I was chanting in my mind. I stood with the bowl in my hand waiting my turn. Out of the corner of my eye, I saw the witch lady coming right towards me, her mouth all full of darkness and her lips painted dark-red like blood. She was wearing the same rumpled dress and her hair was all that you would expect a witch's hair to look like. She stopped right in front of me and, without batting an eyelid, began her tirade of language and obscenities. Only this time she yelled them directly at me. I could not believe that this was happening once more. This was a centre of peace and I had come here to be quiet and reflect. I threw my bowl down and the noise of my own anger filled the room as I ran from that space towards the door.

As I reached the exit a monk stopped me and asked, 'What is wrong?' I was so filled with rage I couldn't even speak. He said 'Let us walk,' and I, like an obedient child, followed him outside. We walked towards the temple. I was dragging my feet, feeling like I was five years old and hurt because of so many things. He motioned for me to sit down beside him and I did.

He smiled a kindly smile and said, 'Where is she in you?' I began to tell him no, how could he even think that. Again he smiled and said 'Where is she in you?' I took a breath as if to steel myself and, before I could open my mouth, he repeated the question very softly, 'Where is she in you?' I closed my eyes and the tears welled up and spilled onto my cheeks. Hot salty and so old. Tears that had been repressed for so long finally finding a way and a reason to be spent. I couldn't breathe and I felt him hand me a tissue. 'There,

REIKI FOR THE SOUL

have you found her?' he asked. I said 'Yes, you see my mother is an alcoholic and many times I saw her in this disturbed state. She was angry at the world and always at the most inopportune time would act crazy. She reminds me of my mother.'

He smiled and said again 'Where is she in you?' I looked into those wise and patient eyes and said, 'She is my worst fear about myself. I am afraid that I will turn out just like her and just like my mother.' At that moment a burden had been lifted off my chest as I sat in a quiet space with the monk. Slowly the time came for us to leave and I walked back to the centre for my class.

In the afternoon and night and into the following day I looked for the woman. She was not there. I asked the monk when I was leaving if the woman was still there. He said, 'Oh yes, she is a patient here. But you do not need to see her any more. You brought her into your life to bring you closer to your divinity. Her work is finished with you.'

I did not know when I decided to go to the centre that people with severe mental problems were residents there and that the monks worked with them. I had my prayer answered and I was ready to see a brighter picture of myself.

Think back over time and see if you can name some of the people who were your mirrors. What qualities, both good and bad, did they mirror back to you? Did you recognize any of the deepest fears you had not dealt with regarding yourself?

I remember…

_____

_____

_____

_____

Life will also give you circumstances in which you will be able to see yourself reflected back. When the going gets tough it is hard to say that the outside world is our reflection. We would rather only own that when times are good. It is very easy to see what is being reflected back to someone else, but for us – well, it can be a different story.

Not Me! I am Only Frustrated

I remember the day well. I had driven into Prague on a crisp autumn day to visit a friend and spend some time with her. She is a high-level executive and works under constant stress all the time. Normally she can handle it, but there had been extenuating circumstances that had caused her to be angry and she was almost eaten up with the anger when I arrived. One of the things I enjoy so much about Mary is that I have an opportunity to discuss many subjects in English, my native language. We are both interested in the metaphysical, and see that we have been given incredible opportunities to be at the forefront of change in this country. She was so angry that, by the time I had taken off my coat and sat down, I could feel the rage in her. It was about work. Everyone was demanding so much of her time and she did not feel appreciated at all. She had been working virtually seven days a week for years and now it seemed they wanted more from her. She was physically tired which made it harder for her to be objective. She was ready to quit her job. I sat with her for a few minutes while she let it all out and the tears came. I said 'What is it you are most unhappy with?' She thought for a while and said, 'I am tired of everyone's anger. They just seem to be pushing me all the time. They shout at each other and me. They blow up at the slightest provocation. No one can keep their cool any more. I guess I am the only one who can cope. And now I am less able to.' She went on to relate several incidents at work that all gave good reasons for her to feel the way she did. I asked her if she was angry. 'No,' she replied. 'I am frustrated with my life.'

She was about to take a trip to London in the next few weeks so I suggested she do a Life Training seminar while she was there. I thought it might help her to hear her mind's accusations and make different choices. I told her it was an important decision in my life to take the seminar and that it helped me so much. Three weeks later I had a call from her and she said that she had done the training when she was in London and wanted to talk to me about it. Could I come to Prague anytime soon, as she wanted to talk to me in person about her experiences? I was filled with hope that the training had given her a new lease of life. When I arrived at her flat I discovered something quite different. She'd had a bad experience. It seemed that she felt the trainers were unfair to the people and pushed them too hard. She thought that some of them behaved in an unjust

REIKI FOR THE SOUL

way. I asked her if she brought this up during the course. She said, 'No, I was so upset at the time I did not want to interact with them.' I then asked her how work was going. Were there any changes in the way people were behaving towards her. Again, there was no change. All she was met with was anger and unfairness in every direction. I gave her some things to look at, a book to read that I thought might help and said I thought it would be good for her to do some dancing or singing to get part of the energy out of her. Not soft dancing but African dancing moving to drums. 'Mary, you simply must move your body,' I said as I gave her a hug at the door.

I was thinking, as I drove back to my home in Liberec, how sad it was that she did not see her own anger. Life was continuing to show it to her in practically every way she looked and yet she denied it. I was imagining how it must feel to have to cope and not let the rage out. I also started to imagine where in her body the feelings of anger would be. I started to feel an incredible pressure in me as I went through this exercise, feeling waves of anger and frustration building in me. It became so intense I pulled my car off to a car park and tried breathing the pressure away. I started seeing recent events in my own life where I had been frustrated. I looked at the parallel of Mary's life and my own. Working all the time, feeling pushed by life. People wanting more than I had energy to give. I started to laugh. My goodness! I had been seeing myself all this time. I had to hear about someone else's problems to get the message. I had been coping, denying my own anger and frustration, and it was not until I started to have emotional identification with her that I began to feel myself. No wonder there were so many angry people around me in these moments. They were reflecting back to me.

Think back over the past several months. What has the recurring theme been with the people in your life? What has been going on at work? Have you been listening to people with the same sort of problems? What do you think life is trying to tell you and have you been listening?

_____

_____

_____

_____

An Inner Dialogue

Today I awoke to a blue sky and a promise of spring around a soft and near corner. The air is clean after days of showers and darkness. After giving myself a Reiki treatment I sat down with my hot water and lemon and decided to meditate. Well, actually, it is like an internal conversation with myself. I ask questions and sometimes I get answers. There are times when I hear the silence and go into that, knowing I am connecting to others and myself in a deep place I call oneness. So I sat quietly and blessed my day. I gave thanks for a good rest and dreams of people near to me in my heart. I was willing for whatever happened to be there.

'Super!' my mind exclaimed. 'I am not going to get a shopping list or things I have to do today. This is the question-and-answer space.' I asked, 'How and why do I fall out of relationship with myself?'

What does falling look like to you, dear one? Is it something you have thrown down or do you suppose I in some way have helped you to fall away from yourself?

No, I own that I have forgotten to be in relationship with myself. This is not something you have helped me with.

And if you fall, does that mean there is no relationship, or that the relationship has changed from the way you have intended it to be?

Yes, I see what you are saying. I am always in relationship with myself, it is just that I have put myself at the back of the line again.

And why is this so, dear heart? Are you too busy to take the time for you? Why are you judging yourself again? Are you truly at the back of the line? Let us look at this simple dynamic. You sat in quiet contemplation. Who are you contemplating for? Why are you meditating or talking to me, whom you call your inner self?

Well, I see your point. I was doing that for myself. I was wanting answers and still do for that matter, yet I see that I have a narrow way of looking at things and you are showing me another way. OK, I agree I am in this moment. I am first in line.

Is it important to be first? And if you are first then who is second and third? Can all relationships be first, is it possible?

Oh no, don't go trying to confuse me now. I have been struggling to keep in relationship with myself and now you ask this question, can they all be first?

And behold; see what you did with the question. You once again said it was a struggle to stay in relationship with yourself. I want you to remember you are always in relationship with you and everyone else. Now, is it the type of relationship you want that is the real question? And do stop struggling so much. Remember the struggle is the ego. Surrender into the flow of life and then you will see yourself right next to all the others and equal to each other.

Why do I do that? I go through this entire struggle to find what is apparently in front of my nose. Why can't I see?

It is simply too easy for you to believe that you can see and moreover have all your answers. You do see and feel the truth, your truth. What you lack is the trust to believe that you know and also that it doesn't have to be so hard. Apparently, you think things need to be hard to be good. And, as well, the struggle you experience is in giving up your ego and surrendering into God, if you like. Much like you surrender into a quiet place to talk to me. You have come to trust our talks and find them helpful. You also are now taking responsibility for the messages you are given. Before, if things that we had talked about didn't go right, you would blame me. But, who am I, dear child?

Well, you know that I understand we are one and the same. I call you grandmother. You are a wise soul I find you a comfort to be with and I appreciate your support and have through the years. You have called me your daughter, Morning Star. While we have different names I am wise enough to know that it is all the same. You are me, I am you, and we are one.

Correct, and that wisdom that you hold as grandmother is yours as well. The relationship that you are striving for is to be in a relationship similar to the one you have with me. You can honour and respect yourself for the knowledge and wisdom you have and for the way you work with people. You then would see yourself as others see you, magnificent. But that is hard for you to accept. It is better for you to see yourself smaller than I. But, dear one, God did not birth light into you for you to play small in the world. No one's destiny is to do that. You are afraid of your power, not of being powerless. If you saw yourself as I do, what a beautiful picture that would be. What would you have to give up to see yourself this way?

My smallness and my judgements about myself.

Exactly, and you are so forgiving of others, why is it so hard to forgive yourself?

You caught me again. We have been in this place before. Many times, in fact, and I am at a loss to answer why I do not forgive myself.

Shall I give you a hint, dear child? If you forgave yourself then what you would have is a clean slate to write you on. It would have space to create. And what would the fear be if the slate were clean?

That what I would create wouldn't be good enough, and quite possibly I would end up repeating the same mistakes over and over again.

And if you did you could forgive again. Or you could be awake enough to feel when you were out of context with your vision. If you use all of you to create then when something begins to change you can feel and see what it is. You can course correct. You have the power and the heart to do this. You must take full responsibility for what you create. I ask you, are we really the same? Do you hold all are one truly in your heart of hearts?

Yes, grandmother, I do.

Well then my child, if I am you and God is you why can't you forgive us who are the same as you? Do you really see that you have not fully integrated this concept of oneness and that by not forgiving yourself you hold yourself out of the light and unity of all? Let this be your task for this time to dissolve the aspect that separates us. Take your time, for we are in no rush. We hold you in this sameness and are waiting for you to just take a step across to join with us. It is yet another initiation of the spirit.

I became aware of the sun-filled room again and the wetness of the tears that had fallen on my cheeks. I could still hear her words echoing in my mind. I stretched, took a breath, and sighed. As I stood up and began to walk from the room I said, 'I will work on this, I promise … but, why does it have to be so hard?'

Really Mari, you have forgotten already!

Have you had an inner conversation with your higher self or God and been shown what your next course of action may be? What did you do with the information? When was the last time you listened and what was the message?

_____

_____

_____

_____

After answering the questions, take time to sit quietly and feel your body. Remember that revisiting areas of your life may also bring up emotions that you may not have expressed in a long time. Take the time to give yourself a self-treatment. By loving into yourself you set these emotions free and acknowledge the importance of each step you have taken.

Close your eyes and take a deep, cleansing breath. Feel your body. Are there areas that are tight or heavy? Are there places in you that need to be touched and loved into? Use your hands to touch these places. Give yourself Reiki to return these areas into harmony. If you have been initiated into Reiki two energy, use the power and emotional mental symbols to work deeply to return yourself to a state of inner harmony and peace.

Honour yourself and your journey thus far.

THE DOORWAY OF
OUR PARENTS

Nᴏᴛ too long ago I was looking at a photo of my parents from early in their marriage. I believe I had been born by then. They were standing by a pond in front of their house, holding on to each other. They looked so happy. My dad was so good-looking I realized why my mom couldn't resist him when they were dating. And my mom was stunning. They looked like models in a magazine. I began to wonder what attracted them to each other and what it was that held their marriage together for many years. They divorced when I was 21.

I remember the bad times in their relationship. That filled many chapters of my adolescence. But I couldn't help but wonder who they really were on the day the photo was taken. What were their dreams? How did they see their relationship? What were the silent expectations they wanted to be fulfilled? Did they talk about these things? I had so many questions as I looked into the eyes of my parents in the photo.

They met right at the end of the war; they lived in the same town. My mom's parents were upper class. They had been part of the original families that founded the city, way back when the wagon trains were crossing the Rocky Mountains. My dad came from the other side of town. I know my grandmother was very upset that my mom was dating, and eventually married, him. Now, when I think about my life with them, aspects of who they were individually come through me. I have heard we are here to bring their vibration higher. Many times we reach new heights that our parents did not in their lifetimes. I believe that fundamentally in some way this is true. We are our own individual expression but our parents' energy has flavoured us.

How do we reach an understanding with our parents? I have decided it takes accepting them just they way they are, not how we wanted them to be. That is a true task, and to do this we need to accept ourselves, especially the aspects of us that are similar to our parents. Also, to have an open door with them, each feeling free enough to come and go like the gentle winds of time. It is like an embrace without limitations and, if we are lucky, this can occur while they are still alive. And, if not, it is my hope we can find this before we ourselves pass on.

When I was little I was so taken by my mother. I thought she was the most beautiful person in the world. I would love to sit and watch her brush her hair and put on her make-up. I remember saying I wanted to be just like her when I grew up. When I was in the fourth grade I realized that my mother was emotionally ill. She had a deep depression that she covered up with drinking. My dad was in the Airforce at the time and we were stationed in Tripoli, North Africa. She was, for the most part, emotionally unavailable for us. For whatever her reasons, I felt a deep fracture in our relationship. It was during this time that I started becoming my mother's caretaker and my childhood essentially ended.

When we came back to the United States we moved for a short while to California where we stayed with my grandmother. Later I was told that my parents had separated. Eventually we moved back together to Maryland. My dad travelled a great deal and my mother's depression and alcoholism were in full bloom. I had decided that I no longer wanted to be like my mother. In fact, I was afraid I would be like her. I never knew until much later that the early decisions I had made during this time were to be such an influence on my life. I also could not really experience my mother any other way but weak from that time on. I became her mother, and in this role-reversal I also had to be in control. This was a behaviour that has gradually been chipped away through the constant use of Reiki and therapy.

All during this time and into my teen years the constant strain of watching out for mom and her behaviour took its toll on me emotionally. I was an introverted young woman with very few friends. I seemed always to be on the outside looking in at life, afraid to be a participant. Branded the black sheep of the family, I made choices in my life that would cause the family to pull together. Now I realize I had made myself responsible and guilty at the same time. Looking back, I wonder how much of the same pattern I repeated that had also been my mother's. All through her life she would remark that the only thing she wanted was her mother to love her and tell her she was loved. She longed for her approval. This was our pattern as well.

I had been living in the Czech Republic for three years and away from the States for five years. I called my mom one evening to tell her I was moving into a nicer flat and that my first book was being published. She was very quiet and said, 'When you were a little girl you told me you wanted to be a doctor. I told you that little girls could not be doctors but nurses instead. You gave up your dream because of that. When you left the States I accused you of running away. Perhaps that is true. What I am aware of is that you have gone to do what your heart had wanted to do since you were little. It didn't matter if I approved or not. You have been willing to lose everything and everybody to follow your heart. You are a doctor, a doctor of souls. I am jealous of you.' That was the first time my mom had acknowledged my work or me. I sat in stunned silence as she told me this. I have often wondered what she wanted to do in her life, what dream she had that perhaps was not fulfilled. What if she had followed her heart? Perhaps I would not even have been born as her life would have taken such a different turn.

I wanted desperately to have a mother who would mother me. I wanted to be the little girl. When my mother died almost two years ago I sat with a woman who had nursed her during the last months of her life. What she said helped me to see my mother in an entirely different light. She told me that my mom wanted so much to be able to mother me and take care of me, but that I was so independent she could not. It was a source of great sorrow for her that we could not go back to the place where this fracture had occurred and switch roles again.

What I am grateful for is that I was able to sit beside her and give her Reiki as she took her last breath. I felt so much love and compassion for this woman who had given birth to me. I was grateful we'd had the time to clear so many things in our life. I was able to let her go and be filled with grace as she went back to the light.

The last piece in my recovery and movement back into relationship with my mom was those words about her wanting to mother me. I realized the deepest cost of my independence was that I caused the space to be there due to my expectations that were not met. I could now heal my inner child and set her and my mother free. I did have a mother who was beautiful, understanding, talented and loving. I am so grateful for being able to see her as she was, not only as my mind had seen her.

I had no idea the profound effect her death was to play in my life. All the reasons to be independent were gone. My life was shaken from the inside out. I had no structure to stand on and now had to work to heal in a deep way. This has happened since her death. I have noticed that I am softer and gentler to myself. I am more available to others and willing to own my stuff. I feel her mothering presence around me. It has also affected the way I mother my own child. My mother's death has been like a rebirth for me. And a birth of a different way to see my mother and hold the memories of her in my heart.

Did you have any expectations of how your mother should have been? What part of your energy is still tied to these expectations and how has it affected your own life and that of your ability to parent?

_____

_____

_____

_____

What are the qualities you admire most about your mother? Do you have these qualities as well?

What will you do to heal the hurt inside regarding your mother, so that you can move from the past into a loving now and future?

_____

_____

My Dad is still alive. I am hoping that we will take the time to come into a deeper understanding and acceptance of each other. When I was little I was Dad's little princess. I would look forward to him coming home so I could be wrapped in his loving arms and made to feel special and loved. His arms were the solace I sought when I felt separated from my mom.

I do not remember at what age that changed and I ceased to be the princess. My guess is that it was when I reached puberty, at the same time I told myself there would be no 'happy ever after' in my life. It has been wrapped up with all the problems they were experiencing with each other. Looking back I understand that children take the blame for the problems of the parents. I thought that the reason Daddy travelled so much was to be away from me.

I did not seem to measure up to their expectations of me. I always fell short of the mark. It is so easy to parent as we were parented. I wish I had the wisdom when I was young to see that most of what I was given was because he had received it the same way.

In hindsight, it is easier to be forgiving and to see the wounded boy in my father. When he is gruff and belligerent he is actually the most wounded. His reactions are deep-seated. How I wish he could set himself free from this. To stand in front of a roaring lion and not be afraid, to pour love into him so that he turns into a kitten takes an act of bravery. Although I feel I am brave in most cases, I have an automatic flight button that is activated when he starts to roar.

I have been sending Reiki to this situation for some time. Losing one parent also puts you in touch with the probable loss of the other. I would like to return to the gentleness with my Dad. To experience his loving side and be able to trust this will stay.

'What will I have to give up to do this?' I am asking myself? The answer is my fear. My fear also keeps me from reaching out to him. I am reminded of the tarot card 'Strength'. The woman reaches into the mouth of the lion. She is fearless. Because she does not have fear and sees the lion as he is and accepts him, she has access to a different depth of him, his gentleness.

Just because I am writing this book about using Reiki to cross through doors to inner peace, it does not mean that I have my life handled. What I hope I am conveying is that because of Reiki I have been moving closer to resolution in many areas of my life. I use Reiki to choose life and to live magically. Part of the choices I am able to make as I come into harmony is to come back into supportive relationships in all areas of my life, including this one.

Recently I was in a group of people discussing how we feel when we are on our own versus when we are with our parents. We have moved away, had our own families and many of us are already grandparents, yet when we come back home and stay with our own parents we immediately feel small. At first we thought that our parents could only see us as their children. We were still blaming them instead of taking responsibility for what gets created. I now feel that it is we who hold ourselves that way. If we came home as the adult wanting to be in an adult relationship with our parents it would be different. But, because we have unfinished business or issues that remain unresolved, we step back energetically to the ages of the particular fractures in our relationship and pick up where we left off. We continue to play the role out until we change something in ourselves.

What is also apparent is that we continue to pass down the same traits in the generations until we do something to change the energetic pattern. The last time I was with my Dad I found myself defending my daughter's behaviour. What my daughter has chosen over time to do is not be around him because he is so judgemental and unforgiving. She feels that no matter what she does she will be wrong or inadequate in his eyes. Where as I stayed, she has chosen not be close to him, as it does not support her living.

We have talked about the probability that her grandfather had a childhood that was less than he needed. Perhaps his demand for others to be perfect reflects his need to be perfect as well. He uses the same yardstick to measure himself as he does to measure others. We have also discussed the probability that when her grandfather is the hardest to be around it is more than likely because there is a little boy inside him that is needing attention and love. I think that in her own parenting she is starting to see this as a real possibility. Our children teach us so much about how we live our lives if we pay attention.

Of course, it is easier to divorce your grandparents than your parents. The problem is that my dad's expectations about how his children and grandchildren should be do not always coincide with our expectations or demands. And, interestingly enough, when we do feel the energetic pressure of having to be a certain way, very often we will react in a way that is the opposite of how we should be. We operate out of a pre-set picture of what we need, and expect others to bring it to us. So we have a statement such as, 'I know how fathers and grandfathers should be, and you are not acting according to my picture.' What we have is a collision of realities. Both the expectations and demands put us straight on a collision course. It becomes a continual no-win situation for all concerned.

When I was little, I said I did not want to be like my mother, nor would I marry a man like my father. What I came to realize over time was that, in relationships, I was choosing to be like my father and marry men like my mother. We bring our unfinished business into our partnerships. The only way to handle this is to come back into relationship with our parents, to clear the past so we can move into today and create from that space.

How we move back into this space will be as varied as there are people in the world for there is no one answer. What I do know from working with this issue myself and also working with others who have had similar problems is that to acknowledge that as long as we do have unfinished business within the family dynamic we will bring this into our current relationships to heal. Often times our bosses or authority figures in our lives take the 'heat' for this aspect that has no present resolution. Even if we feel differently about our parents than when the original fractures occurred, if we have buried resentment, pain or guilt it will have a tendency to show up in the relationships we have now with others.

Once you have realized that what is occurring is often times a pattern in your life, it can ease the dynamic that is going on between you and the one you seem to have this problem with. You can then bring your attention back to the place where it is needed to heal, inside yourself. Once you take responsibility for yourself, you can literally bring light to the situation.

I often use the feeling in my body to help identify problem areas in my life. Let's say, for instance, that I felt abused as a child. I would go inside and feel all the feelings associated with abuse. Where is my body storing the pain and anger and what does it feel like? I also become aware of what my accusing mind is saying by listening to my judgements about my parents, myself and how I must be in the world in order to survive. Then I do the same thing with my current relationships. Does the chatter of my mind have the same accusations? Are the feelings in my body similar if not the same as when I was a child? If so, the chances are that I am repeating a childhood pattern and I am acting out of past reaction. I then work with the feelings. I respond to those areas with Reiki. It is like putting love and light into areas that have been frozen in time. My body relaxes, my mind becomes still and I am far more objective to my present relationships. I can then choose to be 'Here and Now' with them. I also talk to them about what is going on for me. I own my reaction and tell them I had projected my parental disharmony onto our relationship, and possibly one more time. I ask for support and forgiveness.

Communication becomes the key to crossing the threshold of the door. Being aware that you have unfinished business also allows you access to the doorway to your parents. You have taken responsibility for yourself and you stand differently in relationship to them.

Not long ago I had an inner dialogue with 'grandmother' about my parents. I was asking for clarity about my inner process before writing this chapter of the book. She said:

Your parents birth you, but are not your parents because of this. The term parent implies that they pair with you, giving you support, love and respect. You do not owe respect to the ones who birthed you. Rather, you come to respect them for truly parenting you and giving you a healthy life philosophy. If you have had an abusive parent, perhaps by your willingness to understand the seeds of their need to abuse, it will be taken as an act of love on your part. This act of love can also be a step to reconciliation. You always have choice to be in or out of relationship with your birth parents.

The truest act of parenting is to see your child as a gift from God that has been loaned to you for a period of time. We nourish this gift by giving the child space to explore and come into an understanding of how truly precious and loved they are. Very often, when we become parents, we find ourselves behaving towards our children in the same manner our parents did to us. Family parenting patterns are passed down through generations. If you did not like how you were parented then forgiveness becomes the key to unlock the door of the hurt heart. You are better able to be a different parent than you were or expected to be when you have forgiven and moved on in your life.

I have been doing some work around my anger and my reaction to my father's anger. Now there is such a mirror for me to see and experience with him. What I have come to realize is that my anger has been a form of control in order to get other people to do what I want them to do and to have my needs met in any given situation by doing it my way. In this I feel more happy and secure when I am in control. When I am angry I am justified in feeling and acting this way because the other person is to blame for my feelings. It is a form of immaturity that has blocked my ability to listen, respond and to change. I am self-righteous. Either my anger is manifested as a direct attack towards another or lies hidden in a passive aggression or withdrawal, either by complaining or suffering, and all are forms of being in control. I asked myself why I needed to be in control. What was I afraid would happen if I lost control? The answer was that I would be hurt or I would hurt others. I felt this fear, allowed it to build in my body and then responded to it with Reiki, bringing love and light into the darkened and fractured areas of my life. Once the energy had been cleared I could see that my dad was probably reacting in a very similar way out of his own childhood. He learned from an early age that aggression and anger kept him safe from being hurt. What he may not have learned is the cost of continuing this behaviour.

For, even if you win the control game, you eventually lose because when your partner loses they become less attractive to you. They are imperfect. By having an unattractive or imperfect partner you often turn your back on them and you lose as well. I believe that is the principal cause of divorce in the world. We do not fully understand the power game we play out from unresolved childhood fracturing. We project this unfinished business on our partners, making them wrong and not taking responsibility for ourselves. They fail to live up to our expectations and then we can divorce as it is simply too much to work through. If we do not wake up to our behaviour and continue to bring the same circumstances into our lives we will simply have more than one principal relationship and divorce more than once.

Reiki has been instrumental in working through my parental issues. I have also been blessed to do some beautiful work to learn to listen to my mind and tell the truth.

I found the foundation of this work in the 'Life Training'. The Life Training programme is offered in many places throughout the world and is an excellent way to start the process of transforming your life.

I am a long way along the road towards resolution and freedom regarding my relationship with my parents. I am more willing to see my dad and mom truthfully and accept them. I am coming to terms with what is in me that is the same and making choices to resolve my inner conflicts. I am on my way home.

Regarding your father, what was the single most meaningful aspect that he has passed on to you and why do you regard this so?

What do you wish for your dad to realize? Could the same thing be said of you?

Can you imagine what your dad's life was like as a boy? What do you think he needed the most?

Are you willing to heal your relationship if necessary, and what is the first step?

_____

_____

_____

_____

What are you most grateful for in regards to your dad?

_____

_____

_____

_____

If you are a parent, what have you possibly passed on to your children and grand-children that is a family pattern? Are you willing to make resolution now so this can change?

_____

_____

_____

_____

What will it take to forgive your parents and yourself so you can fully embrace life?

_____

_____

_____

_____

Will you forgive them and yourself now, and what does it feel like?

_____

_____

_____

_____

After answering the questions, take time to sit quietly and feel your body. Remember that revisiting areas of your life may also bring up emotions that you may not have expressed in a long time. Take the time to give yourself a self-treatment. By loving into yourself you set these emotions free and acknowledge the importance of each step you have taken.

Close your eyes and take a deep, cleansing breath. Feel your body. Are there areas that are tight or heavy? Are there places in you that need to be touched and loved into? Use your hands to touch these places. Give yourself Reiki to return these areas into harmony. If you have been initiated into Reiki two energy, use the power and emotional mental symbols to work deeply to return yourself to a state of inner harmony and peace.

Honour yourself and your journey thus far.

霊

気

THE DOORWAY OF OUR
EXTENDED FAMILY

EXTENDED family includes grandparents, aunts, uncles, cousins, brothers, sisters and our children. I come from a rather small family. However, they have been a source of growth and inspiration for me. They represent a large doorway I have crossed through to realize inner harmony. I hope you find something to touch your heart through their stories.

From the time I could remember I had certain memories about my grandparents. On my mother's side of the family there was my granddad, George Shuburgh. He died when I was a little girl but I remember two things about him. I sat on his lap and turned the grinder handle to grind the coffee in the mornings when we were staying with them in California. It was a ritual, something to look forward to. I was the chosen child, the first one to do this. I felt special and loved in the kitchen with the sun streaming through the kitchen window and the smell of the coffee beans being ground up. The other was his incredible patience. He would follow me around answering all my questions such as, 'What is this?' 'What does it do?' 'Why?'. He never stopped playing this game with me. He encouraged my natural need to know and I felt so loved in his quiet presence. Years later I asked my grandmother if I could have the grinder, as it was my touchstone to my granddad. Tears welled up in her eyes when she realized that it was my one memory from a house filled to the brim with antiques. She told me that she had sold it years before. That same year my husband and my daughter found one just like it and gave it to me for Christmas. It is often funny what reminds us of our past and our grandparents.

My grandmother, Georgia Shuburgh, was never close to me. She was very reserved and did not hold, hug or kiss anyone. My brother had always been her favourite; she doted on him all the time. I had decided that granddad was mine and my brother had grandmother. I never could figure out how to get her to love me. I felt I had to earn her love. I tried various ways all through my life. My first thought was that I reminded her of my father and that as she did not like the fact that mom had married him, it was a good excuse to reject me.

Now I understand my grandmother at deeper level. I also know that our relationship was reflected through her relationship with my mother. I believe that my grandmother was not shown affection when she was a child. She had not been shown how to love. Her mother was a widow but also a successful businesswoman. In those days not many women were in business for themselves. So my mother was raised in a Victorian household with a governess and, I imagine, a mostly absentee mother.

When grams raised my mom, her favourite expression was 'children are seen but not heard'. I have often wondered how many generations have passed this expectation down and just how many children have bought this way of being lock, stock and barrel. I certainly heard this and knew to be very silent when other people were close to me, especially grown-ups.

Because grams was so upset with my mother's decision to marry my father, she told my mom that as long as she was living, mother would never get anything of value from the house. Mother was an only child. It was expected that when her parents died she would inherit everything and this was the case. However, for as long as grams lived, my mother was not given anything, yet my parents divorced when I was 21. This hurt my mother greatly and helped to reinforce a deep belief she had that her value was measured in how many family treasures you had been given or had been passed down to you. What is also interesting to note is that my mother considered that I had married beneath my station in life when I was 18. I was not given family things from the house either. When we do not wake up to family patterning we keep repeating the pattern with our children. What a heritage we pass down through the generations. Fortunately,

I have now decided my value and that of my child is measured differently. Self-esteem is developed within the individual, not by what we have.

A few weeks after my daughter Stacey had given birth to her first child, Jeremy, I asked her if I could keep him for the weekend. It was to be our bonding time. I took Jeremy over to the nursing home where my grandmother was living to meet his great-great-grandmother. I had him in a papoose nestled up to the front of me. It felt so good to be close to him in this way. When I entered the room grams looked up and I said, 'I have someone to see you.' I placed Jeremy in her arms and she held him with tears in her eyes. She said, 'He is the fifth generation living in our family and an important person to us all.' We talked about the generations that have followed her and what she wanted all of us to know and feel. She said she wanted Jeremy to be proud of where he came from and to realize that people can be wrong and it is OK. When we were leaving I said, 'I love you grams.' I never expected an answer. However, I heard a soft-spoken 'I love you too,' as I walked out the door. It shocked me so much to hear the words I had wanted to hear all those years that I popped my head back through the door and asked her, 'Did I hear you say I love you too?' She smiled and said, 'Yes, I don't know why I didn't tell you years ago. I do love you very much and thank you for bringing me such a lovely present.'

We had moved my grandmother from Long Beach, California to Houston, Texas when her health failed in 1973. The family home that was filled with four generations of memories was sold. I had personally packed all those things that had become the measure of success in numerous boxes. They were moved and most of them were never opened until my mother died in late 1997. By then they had travelled from California, rested in two places in Texas and ended up in Connecticut in my brother's garage. I unpacked them the week after my mom passed away. We were faced with our heritage spilling out of boxes and yet my brother Scott and I realized that the most precious heritage was the two women who had come before us. That was the basis of the family. I have a desk that was my grandfather's and a vase that had been my mom's. What I treasure the most are the words 'I love you' from my grandmother. Nothing could equal those words in value, not even the rarest antique.

I am now the grandmother for the family. I pray that because of the inner work I have done and my use of Reiki, the heritage my child and her children will have received and pass down will be love-filled, honouring the past and yet willing to create new from a centred space within themselves.

What memories do you have of your grandmother/s and the houses they lived in?

_____

_____

_____

_____

Did your grandmother/s fulfil needs in you that were not met by your parents, and if so what were these?

_____

_____

_____

_____

What did you enjoy the most about your grandmother/s?

_____

_____

_____

_____

From where you are in your wisdom, what advice would you give your grandmother/s? Could this be the same advice you might give yourself?

_____

_____

_____

_____

Can you see if there has been some repeated family patterning in relationship to your grandmother/s and their children that has been passed down to you? How has this impacted your life?

_____

_____

_____

_____

What was the gift your grandmother/s brought to you, and the gift you have brought to them?

_____

_____

_____

_____

My grampa Perez was my favourite grandparent. He was my dad's father. To me he was the most complete and fascinating individual I knew. He loved, cherished and accepted me as I was. He lived in the same house my dad was raised in, located on California Street in Long Beach, California. One of my silly memories was when he would come over to my grandma Shuburgh's house to visit. Grandmother didn't like him, so she would lock herself in her bedroom until he left. It was a source of amusement to see how long it would take her to disappear and reappear after he left. He always wore a hat and a string tie. He smoked big fat cigars. He would write letters to me and put a dollar in the envelope saying it was for a rainy day. I cannot put my finger on exactly why I felt so close to him, I just did. I loved him with all my heart. I keep a picture of him on my desk in my office. He is holding my hand. I remember feeling safe.

My dad did not enjoy the same relationship with his father as I did. He was closer to his mother who died before I was born. Perhaps grampa showed my dad a different side of him than I saw and experienced. There always seemed to be life and laughter around my grampa Perez. When he came into the room all the lights seemed to come on and I was a fairy princess. When I look back on what their relationship could have been like I imagine that my father was expected to behave in a certain way and toe the line. Perhaps that is why he felt he needed to be perfect in order to be accepted. I do not know. I have wished that my dad could have felt the love and vibrancy of his father and been close to him. It was never to happen.

I remember visiting my dad at his home in Houston in the early '70s, and just offhand he said, 'I have had so much to handle since your grandfather died several months ago.' I was stunned because he never told me. I had no way to have closure with him. I was hurt that he did not go to his father's funeral and that he had not given me the choice to be there. I have done a lot of inner work around this loss and saying goodbye to him, as well as forgiving my dad for not telling me.

It is sometimes hard to understand what motivates others to be or not to be close to their parents or extended family. I see in myself how my early decisions have certainly coloured my life and what it has cost me emotionally by leaving people out of my life for all my good reasons. So the very dynamic that has been played out with my dad and I seemed to have been present with their relationship, another family pattern, and the same dance once more time.

What were some of the things you remember most clearly about your grandfather/s?

_____

_____

_____

_____

Did you have a feeling of safety with your grandfather/s? If so, why? If not, why?

_____

_____

_____

_____

From where you are now with your wisdom, what advice would you give your grandfather/s?

_____

_____

_____

_____

What do you wish your grandfather/s had told you? And what do you wish you had told them?

_____

_____

_____

_____

What was the gift that your grandfather/s brought to you? And the gift you brought to them?

_____

_____

_____

_____

My brother Scott is two years younger than I am. He was named Duncan when he was born, but his fraternity brothers at the University of Maryland gave him the name Scott as a nickname and it just stuck.

Many times I have worked with people who have probed and released emotion around when a sibling was born. I really do not remember my brother's birth. Nor do I feel any trauma around him. To me, he simply seemed always to live with us and to be an integral part of my life. I know that I was an only child for over two years, yet I do not remember any time before Scott. We played a lot together when we were little and spent much time together. My dad was in the Airforce so travelling and moving around naturally caused us to depend on each other for stability.

I was reminded that I had to set a good example for my brother. When we had injections or went to the doctor or dentist I had to go first and was not allowed to cry because then he would. I also felt that I was blamed for things that he did. He seemed to be able to get away with more things than I could. Basically, we had the normal rivalry growing up. Our milk had to be equal in the glasses. We shared ice cream and got our favourite flavour every other time. I loved chocolate and he loved strawberry. We kept very precise records of whose turn it was to choose. There were times when I knew I hated him and he hated me, yet no one better pick on my brother. I would defend him to the end. I believe he would have done the same for me.

What I know is that in his life his reactions to certain circumstances were different to mine so his memories of how we were raised and what happened are also different. When we talk about the past it is easy to see that we had fractures at different times. I felt like an outsider watching the family live. He was very much inside the family dynamic and close to mother.

Often times we acted out the pain that was present in the house. Our role models, our parents, unwittingly showed us what we thought was acceptable and not acceptable behaviour. When I was three I decided not to cry anymore. I became tough and hard on the outside: 'they could not break me'. However, my brother would cry at the first impression of fear. You only had to look at him in a certain way and he would be crying. He learned to survive in a different way. There is no judgement there; we became very different people in the same family. He would hide under the bed and I would stand impassive waiting to be punished.

Our parents did not do much with us. There were no picnics or sports played. We did not have family outings. We visited friends of theirs and played with their children. We became active in scouting and had role models from our teachers and scout leaders. Scott and I played with each other. We created an imaginary world at times. I felt like we took care of each other in harder times.

When we were three and five years old we decided we would run away from home. I don't believe we were motivated by anything other than the sense of adventure. We got a suitcase and started putting things in it for our big escape. The suitcase was in the closet of our bedroom. We needed food, of course, and I remember my brother putting in his favourite cereal and milk. My mother found the suitcase when we were at school and nursery and cried. Needless to say, our plans to run away were abandoned.

When we lived in Tripoli we had this idea to dig a big hole in the ground at the base of the big tree and make a Bugs Bunny house. It would have all the things we needed to be happy. We dug for quite a long while, but abandoned the idea when we realized we would have to dig almost to China to make our house and it was too much work. Besides, there were other fun things to do in the North African sunshine.

While living in Kent Village, Maryland, we had an excruciating summer holiday. It was a big lesson on many levels. My mother had a beautiful mirror that hung at the bottom of the staircase. One day we were called into the house and shown that the mirror had my initials scratched into the surface. Naturally I was accused as I had been going through a period of writing my name on all my things. I denied it. 'No, it wasn't me.' Then, of course, if it wasn't me it had to be HIM. My brother who normally bawled at the drop of a hat said, 'NO, it was not me.'

So it was decided that we would have stay in our room until someone owned up to it. We were not allowed to go outside and play. We had to be with each other in our shared room. You can imagine all the issues that came up. We both spent hours accusing each other of scratching the mirror. Then we moved into begging each other to come forth and admit it so we could be free. We had great moments of quiet resentment. We spent hours each day being dug in about the other needing to be honest and take their medicine. The days rolled past, the antagonism grew. We became mortal enemies and devised ways to get each other to own up to the truth.

I remember thinking, what is all this great fuss about? I will just say I did it, even though I had not. I would take the beating and then be able to be outside. But a more resilient aspect of me hung tight. I was not going to take the blame for something I did not do. Our whole summer that year was spent in the company of each other. We finally gave in and played with each other. We moved out of resentment and anger back into friendship again. We willingly climbed the stairs after breakfast. I think we even forgot about the mirror. At one point we were set free without explanation. I thought at the time that my mother just realized we would not come forth and that we were also accepting the situation and did not feel punished.

Years later I was to learn that a girlfriend of mine had done the deed and, in fact, had come forward towards the end of the summer with her mother and confessed. She said she was jealous of me. I can't even imagine what she would have been jealous of. It was a different sort of summer holiday. What it taught me was that it was OK to stand by my convictions and that I could turn a bad situation into a pleasant one by the way I chose to think and feel. I honestly enjoyed being with my brother. We both had very active imaginations and could keep ourselves busy for hours.

While we were still sharing a room the problem was that I would have to walk through his part of the room to get to my half. There was a hanging bamboo blind that separated the room into two parts, only he had the pulley on his side. The dresser was shared, but was on his side of the room. The carousel where the toys were placed, shared again, was on my side. So if we were upset with each other it was always a source of trouble to put a toe on the other's side. One night we got into a rather heated argument about our spaces. It finally erupted when my brother ran over to my side of the room and announced he was going to kill me because I was driving him crazy. He took the Venetian blind cord and wrapped it around my neck. I did my best Sarah Heartburn number and laid still pretending I was dying. He continued to pull the cord tighter and I just held my breath like it was the end. A few minutes later he walked back to his side of the room and crawled back into bed. After a few minutes he said out loud in a shaky little voice, 'Boy, am I going to be in trouble tomorrow.' Then he went to sleep. We must have been nine and eleven years old then. I still laugh when I remember that he thought he would be in trouble ... tomorrow. I never asked him how he felt when he discovered I was still alive.

We certainly learned from an early age to be dramatic, imaginative and to support each other. We continued to watch out for each other as we grew up.

I think that basically Scott took on the role of rescuer whereas I took on the role of parent. I also mothered him at times. I brought books home to explain to him about sex when he seemed inquisitive and our parents did not talk to us about that subject. For a while it seemed we either loved each other without measure or at times he had joined the ranks of the family who tormented me. However, when I returned home from my honeymoon, having married at 18, he ran and threw his arms around me and was so happy to see me again. I did not live at home any longer so there was no longer any competition between us. Our relationship took on a new dimension.

I moved away from Maryland and did not have much contact with him for years. He still played out the role of rescuer. He married when he was still in college. His wife had major problems in her family and he basically became the knight on the white horse to carry her away. I knew that mom played the victim and martyr, so it was natural for Scott to be drawn to the same type of woman. He did not have a happy marriage. After fathering two boys the marriage ended. However, his stormy relationship with his wife continued for many years, and cost so much emotion and money. So he was working out a different parental energy in his relationship with his wife.

He is happily married now and has a second family of two boys with this wife. I have noticed that at times he speaks just like my dad and can be as fixed in his thoughts. Is there some fracture he is working with concerning dad? We have not talked about it, as the time we have spent together lately involved mother, her illness, her move to my brother's house as well as her death. My brother and I are a rich mixture of both of our parents. Our parents were the main ingredients and our grandparents were like the flavouring. One flavour Scott has received from his heritage is that he does beautiful carpentry work; grandpa Joe was a carpenter and both have done such beautiful things with their hands. We see and experience more family patterns. Hopefully we use these opportunities to release the past pain and embrace a future filled with promise.

At the beginning of 1999 we came together to celebrate our dad's and my birthdays. Scott flew into Houston from his home in the North East, and I in from the Czech Republic.

We immediately fell into our childhood pattern of running away from daddy to be together and play. We went to an antique mall to look around. While Scott was purchasing some things he remarked to the woman that it appeared she was in pain. She agreed, then Scott introduced me as his sister, 'The witch doctor,' he said. 'I don't know exactly what she does, but I had a problem with my shoulder eight years ago, she put her hands on me and it has been fine ever since.' What a lead in to talk about Reiki! I treated her while we were standing there. She said it felt so warm and relaxing. I have such a visual impression when he says I am a witch doctor.

I am grateful that my brother is in my life. I wish we had more time to just be with each other. We are separated by distance, but not by hearts.

If you have a brother/s and/or sister/s what were some of your memories with them?

_____

_____

_____

_____

What do you still wish for your siblings?

_____

_____

_____

_____

What role did you play in her/his/their lives? And did they in yours?

_____

_____

_____

_____

Are you in a clear relationship with your siblings? If not, what must you be willing to do to be in a clear space and return to love?

_____

_____

_____

_____

What is the gift that each individual sibling has brought to you and you to them?

_____

_____

_____

_____

If you could give each sibling some advice what would it be, and would this advice also be appropriate for you?

_____

_____

_____

_____

My daughter Stacey has been the light of my life ever since she was first placed into my arms in 1966. I had been told I could never conceive a child and was quite surprised I was pregnant instead of having a bad flu. Her father and I had been married for three years before she was born. She was a most wanted and loved child.

After her birth our marriage changed. This was not because of Stacey; it was because we were operating from past programming, especially how parents should be.

It seemed to me I became like my parents and he became his. When I say this I am referring to the aspects that needed to be healed in our personal relationships to our parents in regard to parenting and our expectations that were not met. These were now brought forward to heal and thus were exaggerated. We had so much projection towards each other and did not have the basic communication skills to talk about what was going on.

He worked all of the time from morning to night, and while I worked as well, I was home with Stacey alone. We became more like brother and sister than man and wife. Also he was eight years older than I was. I started growing up and we literally grew away from each other. We had nothing in common except Stacey.

So I clung onto this precious child as if she gave me the very reason to live. I understand now I was too close to her, if there is such a thing. I became dependent on her and she to me. She was my breath.

She never met a stranger. She would go to anyone and love him or her. She has always been such a beautifully open and loving girl. When her dad and I would argue I would find her in the back garden crying. I often thought later how sensitive she was to the trouble in the house. I was quite ill most of the time and there were times we were separated because I was in hospital.

Even as I write this I am coming to a deeper understanding of how disharmony in my personal life also gave her opportunities to react in hers. We set in motion so much when we are asleep and so unaware.

I left her father and moved to Houston, Texas. I moved away abruptly. I rented a car and drove across the border between Georgia and Alabama before telling her we were moving away. I was afraid of losing my mind; my physical and emotional pain was so great. Stacey was four-and-a-half. As we crossed into Alabama I said, 'We are moving to Houston. We will stay with grampa Perry till we can have our own place and you will go to school there.' She looked at me and said, 'Good mommie, you won't cry anymore.'

We were in Houston six months when her father flew to Houston and kidnapped her from the nursery school where she stayed during the day. Every December 3rd, I remember two things – the loss of Stacey and her teacher's face when I came to pick her up. I have done so much inner work on this event in my life. I see the pictures without the big emotional charge. It serves to remind me that running away from the problem doesn't work as you bring the problem with you (it is inside), and to communicate, communicate, communicate. Problems cannot be solved in reaction; it takes patience and a willingness to open the depth of you and share what is going on, also accepting voluntarily to having made a mistake and to apologize. I have used second degree Reiki energy to help me to clear this past emotional trauma.

I had to learn to live alone. I was 26 and had never been alone in my life. Stacey had been the centre of my life and my reason to live. It was up to me to make myself the reason. I could not stand to be in the house by myself. I did not sleep. It took months to start accepting myself and to be alone. For so many years I had run from myself. Now I had the time to come into relationship with me. It was a sometimes painful process. I had to deal with the judgements I made about the reasons and myself for not having my daughter there. I had made myself wrong for everything. I was very bitter towards myself and unforgiving. Society had judgements about a mother who did not have her child with her. In order not to be condemned by others I stopped talking about my daughter. At the time I was working as an optician and could not even work with children, as it was too painful.

I was eventually awarded visitation with Stacey in the summers and every other Christmas. I lived my life for those times. I literally put my life on hold till she arrived. The sun was back in my life again. Needless to say, every time she left I would go into such an emotional tailspin that I would end up in hospital. My mind proved to be a willing and strong instrument to create the pain I craved as well as the punishment for being such a bad person and a bad mother. I know these statements are not true now. I did the best I could do; I am a good mother and a good person. This mind chatter that kept coming up was from old fracturing in my own childhood. Often times we make judgements about ourselves when we are very young and then spend the rest of our lives making ourselves right about our beliefs. I had not yet worked enough on myself to forgive.

I remarried when I was 28. Stacey was instrumental in getting us together. She was with us when we decided to marry, get the blood tests, apply for the licence, buy the rings, and for the ceremony. She was the conductor of the whole thing and we followed her lead. Later she told me that she didn't think it was good for me to be alone.

Stacey started talking about her experiences when she was living with her father in

Georgia. It gave us such a fright about her care that we started to investigate her situation there. She also asked if she could come and live with us full time. We applied through the court system, presented our facts and were given custody of Stacey when she was 12 years old. My husband eventually adopted her legally.

One of the most heart-breaking moments in my life was when she came home from school and asked me what was for dinner. I told her what I was fixing and she said 'Ugh!' I replied, 'If that is the biggest mistake I make in my life that will be fine.' She said, 'The biggest mistake you made was when you gave me back to my father.' I turned off the stove and we sat down to talk. I listened to the lies that her dad had told her. She was given to think that all those years I had asked him to come and get her because I did not love her anymore.

Her pain about being separated was compounded by the lie that she was unloved by me. She said when she missed me she would put her head down on the school desk and cry. Her teachers understood. I didn't want to project my issues that I had with her dad onto her so that became the reason I did not communicate about what had happened when we were together. She must have been so confused during those years. I wanted her to have a loving relationship with her father. This has proved to be another lesson in the importance of communication and the expression of feelings.

The Stacey that was kidnapped had been a loving, open child. When she came back to live with us she was troubled and closed. Her life had brought opportunities to her for reaction. How many of her thoughts about herself were similar to mine and even to other generations of the family? That is something to think about, especially since I realize the way we pass things down in the family. It makes me more committed to this work and this way of living.

When Stacey was in High School my marriage with her second father ended. She blamed me for the reason he left, and was so angry with me. She was a teenager with all her issues of puberty and now had to deal with loss again. I was in my own state of grief and instead of pulling together, as had been our previous pattern, we pulled apart. I believe we both felt misunderstood and miserable with each other. I was in survival mode. I was determined to have a stable environment for her by keeping the house so she could also complete school with her friends. I lost my job as well about the same time. Life was increasingly a struggle.

Finally I did a course that helped turn my life around. It was the Life Training. It helped me to see the patterns in my life, listen to my mind's accusations and be truthful. I could see I had been the creator of my life circumstances and I began to take responsibility for what I had created. I also took Reiki. Both set me on my path to freedom.

Stacey thought I had been brainwashed. I was not reacting in my usual way. I did not get plugged into the drama we had so carefully danced to before. She also became resentful that I was not home and was finding a life for myself. I remember thinking that she did not want me to be near her, yet she was angry when I was not there to be angry at! What a web we wove with each other.

Only this past Christmas did we talk more and cry about not being as close as we wanted to be. She had become as independent as I had been at her age. I wanted to mother her, yet she had moved past that. She did not trust me as a mother. She said, 'All the people who love me leave me, even you.' She was referring to me leaving the States and moving to Europe. We did not see each other for seven years. She went through a number of big challenges in her life – divorce and being alone without me. We had fracturing that will take time to heal. I know we are more willing to talk about it. I enjoy holding her and talking. She is such a busy mother of three now that it is quite hard to get her to sit still enough to love into her. I am praying we will continue to clear this part of our lives and come back into the centre. It will free the energy on her children as well. I want my grandchildren to be free of our past. And the same issue that my mother had about wanting to mother me has now manifested in my relationship to Stacey. I want for us to be interdependent, not independent. There is such a cost in being independent, as we cut ourselves off from people. It is protection that is not needed.

She has three beautiful unique children. All are so different and yet I see her in them. Jeremy has her sensitivity. Tanner has her sense of adventure and Jinny has her openness and loving quality. All are headstrong. I imagine she would say that comes from their fathers, but she knows that is a trait on our side of the family as well.

She has developed and maintained a loving relationship with her birth father. It is unfortunate that her second father has not been in her life for some time. It is a loss for both as they were important to each other at one time.

When I think about the gifts she has brought to me over the years, the quality of sunlight and warmth is still the best one. I do not have to be with her to feel the sun. It is always with me, tucked into my heart. I do not need her to be who I am; she continually complements me. Our relationship has changed and continues to mature. I love watching her mother. I enjoy our friendship; I celebrate her joy and stand close to her in her sorrows. I am immensely proud of her. Not for what she has done in her life, but for whom she is as a person. Open, loving and fun to be with. She is still searching for herself. I hope she will see how truly wonderful she is and come to believe in herself as much as I do. I am her biggest cheerleader in life.

What memories do you have of your child/children that could be parallel to your relationship with your own parents?

_____

_____

_____

_____

Can you see yourself in your child/children and what does that look like?

_____

_____

_____

_____

What do you want for yourself in regards to your relationship with your child/children now?

_____

_____

_____

_____

Is there something to forgive in your past regarding you and your child? And if so, when will you do this?

_____

_____

_____

_____

What is the advice you would give your child now, and why would it be important?

_____

_____

_____

_____

What is the gift your child/children have brought to you? What is the gift you have brought to them?

_____

_____

_____

_____

When I finished writing this section about my daughter I closed my eyes and rested back in my chair. I began feeling the familiar feelings of grandmother near. I surrendered into this energy. She wanted to tell me something.

My dear child you have discovered something beautiful in this recollection of your extended family. You are seeing and feeling just how interwoven life is. One cannot assume that a thread can be pulled from a sweater without unravelling the whole work. Your life has been woven with the many colours of the people and happenings in your life. It is your tapestry.

You never remove something to change it. You continue to add to it. When you and others look at what you have woven it has character. Places in the weaving where you are learning lessons may have tighter threads. Then there are times it seems you are sailing through life and that will be reflected too. In order to gain the perspective needed to enjoy all of your life tapestry you must forgive the past. See it as stepping stones to now. Accept that some lessons have been harder and move through them into love. Always keep in mind the gifts that each person has brought to you and be thankful for yet another day to weave your web of life.

As I opened my eyes I clearly saw that the gift grandmother continues to bring me is, Grace.

After answering the questions, take time to sit quietly and feel your body. Remember that revisiting areas of your life may also bring up emotions that you may not have expressed in a long time. Take the time to give yourself a self-treatment. By loving into yourself you set these emotions free and acknowledge the importance of each step you have taken.

Close your eyes and take a deep, cleansing breath. Feel your body. Are there areas that are tight or heavy? Are there places in you that need to be touched and loved into? Use your hands to touch these places. Give yourself Reiki to return these areas into harmony. If you have been initiated into Reiki two energy, use the power and emotional mental symbols to work deeply to return yourself to a state of inner harmony and peace.

Honour yourself and your journey thus far.

霊
気

THE DOORWAY OF
WORK AND PLAY

I TOOK a deep breath and began to relax. The morning was fine like silk resting on my skin; the morning sun was just up and had begun to warm me. I was at the beginning of a new chapter and wanted some insight from grandmother. Sitting comfortably, I asked, 'What words of wisdom do you have about work and play?'

Why do you suppose my wisdom would be better than yours, dear one, when it is you who has a life of experience of playing and working? Or have you allowed yourself to do both?

I sat with her question in my mind and began to feel that her words had indeed stirred something up in me. Well, you know I have been wanting to play, or to learn how to play.

My child you have been saying that for years. When will you allow yourself to play, and what would play look like to you? What would it feel like in your being?

Grandmother, I just wanted your wisdom. I didn't want to think about all this now. I have so much to do. Can I get back to you on this later?

So, my dear, are you playing or working? Is it possible that play and work can actually be one and the same?

You are not letting me get away with anything this morning. I am working and not playing. OK, I see I can simply resist or relax and go with the flow. Going with the flow is then essentially like play as there is no struggle. I imagine that it would then have some relationship to how I am holding work. In this case, if I am tense or struggling, my work is not flowing and thus would not be considered play.

Wonderful, now you are willing to play with me! Is the work you are doing satisfying you? How did you decide to do the work you do, and are you happy doing this now?

Yes, of course I will play with you. But you know your playing is evoking me to come into a realization about myself and that can be work. I had always wanted to help people. I have a strong sense of justice and thought I would like to be a doctor. My decision to do this work stemmed from a personal experience of Reiki treatments bringing me inner peace. World peace and brotherhood have been important to me as it seemed so natural that people having a sense of inner peace could create the peace I was imagining and working for. The decision to do this work was easy because I could see how Reiki could help us to work together to reach this.

At first, because Reiki was so new, I still did not trust I could do what I wanted to support myself in my life. I continued to work in a normal job and did my Reiki in the evenings and the weekends. In fact, this new part of my life was mostly hidden and I lived out two lives that ran parallel to each other. I thought of these parallel lives as normal and 'not normal'. It was fairly easy to keep one foot in each camp, so to speak. That is until what I considered normal didn't feel so comfortable as before. The space between both of these camps was beginning to get further and further apart. Eventually, I made a choice to put both feet down in one space, and that choice was Reiki.

My actual decision to take my first Reiki course was quite different because at that time I was only interested in getting well and had no desire to work with other people. I was searching for a way back to health. Little did I know when I asked for a way to be shown to me, how meaningful the answer would become. My life has literally been transformed since that choice.

Am I happy doing what I do? That is a big question and one that I am doing soul-searching with now. I love Reiki and it is certainly part of my natural rhythm of living. I love teaching Reiki, especially to witness the transformational qualities at work during the time we are together. I love facilitating other personal development courses and writing books. The biggest problem I am facing is that I want to take more of a back seat right now.

What would that look like to take a back seat and why at this point of your life do you feel this as a possible next step?

Basically, so much has happened and I have worked at such a pace over the past 10 years that I have not taken the time I feel I needed to integrate all that has happened and is happening. I have had such big spiritual shifts in the past few years and have worked closely with so many people. I have taught 30,000 people in seven years and have written five books. It seems I need time for all the parts of me to come back together. I have also been introducing new and exciting work that is the combination of all the work I have done.

At first I felt guilty that I wanted to slow down and possibly change direction a bit. Then I worked with my reaction of feeling guilty to see what was under that and found some more issues I had with my own value. The association takes a lot of my time. Now I see that with maturity, I also want to make some changes. When I welcome change I am also sourced. If I stay still I become stagnant. I have been feeling as if I am giving birth to a new Mari. This new Mari needs time to BE and not do. To listen, connect inside and be sourced.

So in other words you want to do your work without being so driven. You want to approach your work again with a sense of play and freedom that you have lost by being so busy. Would you say this is correct?

Absolutely! I had such a great need to help. I was so idealistic I wanted to help save the world. Then it was changed to saving the Czech Republic. I am more realistic. By giving out so much of myself, I in essence left nothing for me. I was burned out. I still could be sourced by my work, but the absolute joy had been lost. The struggle was too great. I was swimming up stream and not surrendering into the flow. At the end of last year I was overwhelmed by life. I realized that I had taken too much on my plate and needed to come back into the centre and feel what makes my heart happy. I also want to balance my personal and work time. I need to be creative, to paint and write and sing. When I am centred I am free and I play. My work and play are then the same.

Can your play be separate from your work, and if so, what would you like to be playing at?

Certainly I would love to have time that I spend playing that is separated from work. And yet have the playfulness in my working. It is a sense of lightness and being centred. As far as what I would love to do to play, I love art galleries, music, books, movies, and being still with friends. I am reminded what one of my spiritual teachers said to me: 'Be still and hear the soft sweet words of God'. I also wish to develop more friendships and be with my friends absolutely, enjoying being together. I mostly want quiet soft space to be with people where I am not the teacher. I am Mari.

You say you have been driven. What makes you drive yourself so much?

When you come right down to it, initially it was to prove that I was good and had a value. I had developed a personality that had striven for perfection. The only problem with that is I never could make it to my idea of perfect. Not only that, I realized that I was using the same measuring-stick and demanded that others be perfect too. It was a no-win situation all around. I was continually driven along to get it right and to prove myself and wanted others to do the same. When I realized what I was doing I started to work on it by using Reiki and other techniques. I have come into harmony with my perfection drama and no longer need to prove myself. However, the need to champion for a cause is strong in me. I find that when I ask myself why I have been so idealistic, the answer always is because I care so much.

What have you learned this morning, dear one, and what wisdom can you share about work and play?

I stretched and yawned as these words felt like petals inside my mind. 'What wisdom can you share…?' The sun had hardly moved at all, yet I felt as if I had spent the day with her. She had pointed me in a direction to write and she had evoked me to remember to share my own wisdom.

Most of us were asked when we were growing up what we wanted to be. Our parents thought it was so cute when they heard 'A mommie just like you' or 'I want to be a fireman'. We are asked to imagine what it is we want to do. Yet when we say this from our heart some of us get a message that it is either silly or not good enough for the future.

As we go through school we are asked to decide how we will spend the rest of our lives working and what we will do to prepare ourselves for this work. I wonder when we forget what our heart is feeling about this choice and rely totally on our minds to make the decision. We often listen to what our parents think would be a good career for us, but do we trust ourselves enough to feel for our answer? At what point do we return to use the gifts we have to do what makes our heart happy? I have noticed when the heart is happy and you are working out of this, the way to be supported naturally comes to you. When we are unhappy there is a struggle and most of the time the earning of money and status is likened to swimming up stream, hard and exhausting.

I am not saying that earning money and using your mind are bad. I believe we are indeed in this world to be fully supported by life and that it is we who block this energy by our reactions. God wants us to prosper. If you have a natural analytical mind you will find a way to marry heart and mind to do what makes your heart sing. Reversibly, when you are sensitive and listen to your mind, you will be drawn into something for which you can use your sensitivity to support yourself. Perhaps you will do work that involves using your hands to create something beautiful.

I remember my first boyfriend in High School. Phil was very talented. He made his own sailing boat. The love he used in its construction was so evident. He studied business at university. I always felt he would be good at whatever he set his mind to. Twenty years later I saw him again and I was so happy to hear that he not only had a successful business but also was now in research to develop artificial blood. He had designed special equipment for filtration. He had found a way to marry his analytical mind and his love of construction to bring forth something to help other people. Phil is successful; not only for the money he is earning but also for his heart-felt contribution. He has his own sailing boat that he and his family enjoy.

Since we spend approximately one third to one half of our day getting to and from work plus working, I would hope that we are doing what we love to do. Yet when we find out we are not, what steps do we take to change the direction in which our work will take us? It is interesting how life will somehow find a way to support us. We may end up laid off from our job and find new doors that open to us in totally different fields and this new venture seems to be 'right up our alley'. Or perhaps it gives us enough time to see that we want to take a different step. We may choose to open a different door and explore what is out there for us. I think it is wonderful to hear stories of high-powered executives who decide to move away from stress-filled jobs and take up something to give themselves and their families a deeper, more meaningful quality of life. In these moments of change we are often called out to do something our heart has longed to do.

I wanted to be a doctor when I grew up. Later it was an artist. I started working when I was 13 years old, book-keeping for a furniture store. I worked on Saturday and Sunday. When I was in High School I had a job as the night manager for a doughnut shop. I had a lot of responsibility at an early age. I was trusted and earned that trust. I also worked as a waitress. At the age of 16 I was made a head waitress as I took on a more responsible role. Then I moved into book-keeping again. It was always a joke in my family because maths was my worst subject. Yet I had a natural leadership quality and took responsibility so I was promoted and often in my life made the head of a department. One day I went to have my eyes tested for glasses. The doctor started asking me what I did in my job, how I related to people and what I wanted to do with my life. I left that day with a prescription for glasses and a new job. I went to work for the doctor as his office manager and his assistant. I finally started getting closer to the medical field. I eventually was trained as his surgical assistant and then he decided I needed a better job with more ability to earn money. He sent me to school to learn to be an optician and to run his two optical shops. I had a very successful career as an optician. I eventually went on to own an exclusive optical shop with a friend. I was considered a leader in the high-fashion eyewear industry.

REIKI FOR THE SOUL

Working with people to help them overcome specific problems was natural to me. I loved being of service. My heart was involved but I was yet to find my true calling from the centre of myself. Eventually, I found Reiki because of being ill. Reiki helped to move me closer to what I would do for my living from my heart. It was still a process of letting go and taking a risk. All the things I did to earn my living from age 13 on had prepared me for this time. I have used all my experience to help me to work with people. The office skills and responsibility trained me to run an organization and make business decisions. I work from my heart and I am supported. As far as the doctor I wanted to be, my mother said before she died 'You are a doctor of the soul'. It all came full circle.

I wonder how many of us are truly working with the gifts that we have either brought to this world or acquired along the way. How many times will we say, 'I do this to make money so that at some time I can do what I love to do'? It is a great pity when someone dies and the family says 'He really hated his work and couldn't wait to retire to do the things he loved. It is a shame he didn't live long enough to do that'. And will we stay caught up in the rat race of making money and not taking the time to enjoy ourselves, thinking there will be another time?

My brother Scott went to university for what seemed like an eternity. He was always changing his major. I believe he was in pre-med., law and finally business. He moved to New York, met his current wife there, and went to work for a defence contractor. The Cold War ended and so did the need for the USA to buy so many defence items. Eventually, his work was phased out. I wondered what he would do. His education was all geared to this type of job. While waiting for a job he began to fill his time remodelling his bathroom and kitchen. The result was so beautiful that people began asking him if he could remodel their house or flat. Out of this experience a new profession was born. He is now a very successful contractor. He uses his hands to create such beautiful kitchens. He is a real craftsman. What I remembered the most about that time was the joy I saw in my brother's eyes when his work was complimented. He was finally using gifts that he brought into the world to do work that gave him immense satisfaction.

Do you remember what you said you wanted to do when you grew up? What was that?

_____

_____

_____

_____

What was your principal work? Was it the same as you wanted or dreamed, and why or why not?

_____

_____

_____

_____

Knowing what you know now in your life, what would you like to do to earn your daily living?

_____

_____

_____

_____

What gifts do you have that you can bring to your work?

_____

_____

_____

_____

I remember when I was a little child it seemed everything was play except school and that wasn't so bad because we had break, lunch and a nap. Gradually, as I grew older and had homework, school was less fun although I did like the challenge of learning several subjects, and besides, my friends were there. I would come home and change clothes and my world would expand. In those days we used our imagination to create a lot of what we did for play. The playground became our fort, a tree, our lookout tower. A pot and pan became our kitchen and the grass and berries were the main ingredients. When we played as a group we had to decide what we would play and who would have the major roles in the play. We were always riding our bikes somewhere. Everything seemed like an adventure. We explored an old house by the railway line. No one had lived there for at least 20 years. Our imagination would run wild creating life as it was then. Sports were impromptu. We played baseball and football as much as we played dolls. I was a tomboy with moments of playing mother and having tea parties. It started to change when I went to Jr. High School at 12.

Puberty seemed to put a different perspective on life. The telephone and the record player were the things play revolved around and it became serious. I was raised during the beginning of rock and roll. Elvis Presley was the dream idol. So many moments were spent listening and sighing, either alone or with friends. Of course, attention turned away from tomboy things to what to wear. We had our standard dress, which consisted of blue jeans, bobby socks and our dad's white shirt. We also wore a circle pin and had a scarf tied around our ponytails. We wanted to be different from our families whom we felt did not understand us and ended up looking just like each other. Boys also became our major preoccupation. I was too young to date, but mom would drive a bunch of us to the movies to see Elvis. If we had boys with us, holding hands and stealing a kiss was heaven.

Competition entered into our play. We had teams in school where there had to be a winner. Although they taught the importance of the team, a lot of emphasis was placed on winning and so sports became serious. We even had a Jr. High School football team.

High School was more of the same. Dating replaced playing after school. If we were lucky enough to date a boy with a car then we would go to the neighbourhood hamburger joint and park outside and hang out. Most of us were working after school so a lot of this depended on the amount of free time we had. Plus many of us had after-school activities that we were involved in. I was in the drill team and we practised our marching most afternoons. The emphasis was placed more on social interaction.

At this time in my life I was feeling very lonely. I did have a boyfriend who had a car. However, both of us worked after school as well and homework took a lot of time. The focus in my life was balancing all these things and still being able to go out on Friday night to the local teen hop sponsored by the school. Music and dancing were still one of the most important things. It was during this time that I pulled back from life. My mother needed my attention more and more. I was confused and troubled. My boyfriend seemed to be my salvation, a rock to lean against in a stormy night. I had few friends as my time was taken up working and studying. I can't remember when I stopped playing or perhaps I just forgot how. What I do remember was life was serious and there was no play. This decision I made in my teens has been following me ever since.

Marriage was a time to work and put my husband through school or to start businesses. Life was a serious affair. We had no time for play. Of course my family, my parents, had the same work ethic. I imagine I was following in the footsteps and along the path that was most familiar at the time. At night we were too tired to play. We wanted to have a better life so had decided to do two jobs to save money. What a serious decision. We never gave ourselves time to live.

When I met my second husband, Ken, he invited me into a different world. He was a photographer and so saw the world through the lens of the camera. He was also very artistic. He gave me permission by being who he was to source that artistic side of myself. I had run away from that to punish my mother who wanted me to be an artist. Now it was laid before my feet to be picked up again. We did many creative things together. He also introduced me to wearing jeans again; sleeping under the stars on the beach. I literally saw the world differently. I met my husband during the time my daughter, who had been kidnapped by my first husband, was living away from me. He brought sunshine into my life and helped me to heal my heart.

When my daughter came to live with us I wanted so desperately to make up for all those lost moments that I became a serious mother. I had stepped onto the well-worn path of my parents again. Ken and Stacey became playmates and I was the serious one. How easy it was to stop being playful, after all, life is supposed to be serious. One time we were at the beach. Stacey and Ken were running up and down dipping occasionally into the water and laughing with delight. They asked me to come and play with them and I did not. I remember thinking 'Someone has to be serious here'.

I began to live my life as if I were the outsider looking in again. This pattern has been one that I had in place for years. By not giving myself permission to be with the group, I also was alone, often times lonelier when there were many people around. Why did this behaviour come into my life? I see now it was how I had to be to survive. It fed into a pattern developed in early childhood. This would haunt me for years and still is an easy one to fall into. It certainly was a factor that worked against us in my marriage. My husband had lost his best friend and playmate and gained a mother instead.

After my divorce my friend Janet and I decided to do some inner child dialogue to help heal some fracturing that we had become aware of in both of us. The intention was that we would spend the weekend at the beach. During all our waking time we would speak in little girl voices and say whatever popped into our minds. We would also play together. I was 40 years old at the time. We were sitting on the sand at the beach digging and making a sandcastle. Little Janet said, 'I don't ever want to grow up.' Little Mari replied, 'Me too, 'cause being big is terrible.' Little Janet said, 'Yea, you don't get to play and life is so serious.' Little Mari said, 'Yes, and you cry a lot.' We spent two days being our little girls. We cried, laughed and played.

On the last day, a couple in their late 60s walked by, watched what we were doing for a while, and walked on. Later they returned and asked if they could play with us. They transformed into children as well. It was a very healing experience and also very enlightening. So many beliefs about how it is to be big came up for us and we also uncovered how we must be in order to survive in the world today. Little Mari will still write to little Janet. We write to each other using our non-dominant hand. It is a process that we enjoy and it still supports us to access a part of us that has a need to be listened to.

Now I am in the Czech Republic and I am realizing that I have created almost the same thing I had in my marriage to Ken. I have married myself to the International Association of Reiki. Life is serious and I must work hard. Someone has to be the Mommie and I have chosen this role. It is one that has become more and more uncomfortable. The past two years have been a time of redefining my role and moving more into harmony within myself. Being a mother, you can also take a role of empowering or disempowering others. When I do too much for people it does not support them to do things for themselves. It also gives me permission not to do things for myself. I can play the martyr. This was the role I was most afraid of. My mother's role was that of a martyr. I had said I would never do that and yet what I discovered was that I had become a bigger one than she ever was.

I have an 'earth mother' quality. The solution to my imbalance has been to move into a better relationship with my sexuality. As I see and experience myself as a woman the mother role comes into harmony. I can empower others and not give myself away. By healing the deepest fractures around being raped and molested as a child, I can be free to also step back a bit, take on new work, and be in partnership. Also it frees me to play. I have moved into the centre of the group and am no longer on the outside looking in.

What do you remember about playing as a child and who were your playmates?

_____

_____

_____

_____

When did things begin to change with regard to play, or did they?

_____

_____

_____

_____

What do you remember about playing with regard to your years around puberty?

_____

_____

_____

_____

Have your ideas about play changed?

_____

_____

_____

_____

Do you allow yourself to play now as much as you would like to, and if not, why?

_____

_____

_____

_____

Have you seen or experienced some patterning from your family that has perhaps hindered your decisions about playing? If so, what have you done to come back into harmony with regard to this?

_____

_____

_____

_____

Do you feel you are balanced in your work and play? If not, can you see things that you will change?

_____

_____

_____

_____

Is there an aspect of play in your work?

_____

_____

_____

_____

After answering the questions, take time to sit quietly and feel your body. Remember that revisiting areas of your life may also bring up emotions that you may not have expressed in a long time. Take the time to give yourself a self-treatment. By loving into yourself you set these emotions free and acknowledge the importance of each step you have taken.

Close your eyes and take a deep, cleansing breath. Feel your body. Are there areas that are tight or heavy? Are there places in you that need to be touched and loved into? Use your hands to touch these places. Give yourself Reiki to return these areas into harmony. If you have been initiated into Reiki two energy, use the power and emotional mental symbols to work deeply to return yourself to a state of inner harmony and peace.

Honour yourself and your journey thus far.

霊
気

THE DOORWAY OF FRIENDS
AND FRIENDSHIP

DURING the many stages of our lives, we make friends. These friends may also represent where we are in our personal development. We are very lucky if we end our life with five of the same friends that we started with. A childhood friend that is with us to the end is a rare and precious thing. Our friends are also people whom we work things out with. They can mirror back to us our majesty and grace or the parts of us that have remained in the darkness, only waiting to be discovered if we choose. They will be people we have something in common with.

In our early childhood our playmates could also be our neighbours or children we went to school with. When I was five years old I was best friends with Nancy. We were in the first grade together. We had many things in common. Both of us had younger brothers and dads who travelled a lot. We would play in her back yard, which was right around the corner and down the street from my house. One of the things we liked to do was watch her neighbour through the fence. We thought it was a silly game because he would walk around without any clothes on. We would giggle about it. I do not know why we did not say anything to our parents about what we saw; it was our little secret.

One day he invited us into his house for cookies. He molested both of us that day. It was one thing in common that both of us were ashamed of for years. I never told my parents about it, nor did Nancy, although we did not go back for cookies again. This incident haunted me throughout many years of my life. I had decided that I was the one who was bad. No one would do this to a good girl. This basic decision was a turning point in my life. As I look back at photos of my childhood, that year was when the light went out of my eyes.

I remember when we moved back to California from Tripoli, North Africa, and I started school midway through term. Friendships had already been formed and lines drawn in the schoolyard. I was a shy child. Because we moved so often I found it hard to make friends, and once I made them it was difficult when we had to move again. When I was introduced to the class at my new school I felt so alone and out of place, certainly not in my comfort zone. At break, a girl named Mandy came up to me and said I could be her friend. I was over the moon, my first day at school and a friend already. As an act of friendship I carried her musical instrument around for her. I would meet her at the corner by my grandmother's house, carry it to school, and back home. Heck, it was such a small price to pay to be her friend. It was a good thing I was a sturdy girl because her instrument was a bass cello.

One day in the school playground someone made fun of Mandy so I punched him in the nose. You see, I was white and she was an African American. Actually, I did not see myself as white. If someone asked what colour I was I would say I was more olive or deep pink. I had never been taught to hate anyone. My dad was in the service where there were many races of people. I have always been a person who just saw an individual, not the colour of their skin. So here I was only a few days in this school knocking someone down because he didn't like Mandy's colour. I walked away trembling. I wasn't normally a violent child. I went up to my friend and told her I was sorry that she had to hear the boy say those things. She smiled and said, 'Mari, you are my best friend.' She picked up her cello and we held hands as we walked from the schoolyard. She never had me carry her cello again.

Being tolerant of people's colour worked in my favour because I had a group of multi-cultural friends. We called ourselves the rainbow tribe. I learned so much about different nationalities first-hand by visiting their homes and eating dinner with them.

On my ninth birthday my grandmother said I could have a party and invite my friends. She very seriously sat me down and asked me if my friends were from good homes and acted nice. She said she didn't want any troublemakers at the party. I assured her that they were wonderful. She would love them as much as I did. She allowed me to take the invitations to school and give them out. On the big day everything was ready in the back garden of her house. My friends started to arrive. Imagine my grandmother's surprise when she exclaimed, 'Mari, you are the only white child here.' I said, 'No, grandmother, I'm not white, I am dark pink.'

I imagine what brought the rainbow tribe together was our differences. What made it even better was the sameness. How I wish I had pictures of that party. Each child gave me something from his or her country as a present. It was truly a very special birthday. Not long ago I was visiting the part of London called China Town. I went into a shop and found the same sort of candy I had been given 45 years ago. It brought all the good memories and feelings back to me. Kim's father had the Chinese laundry two blocks from my Grandmother's house. I would go to pick up the clean laundry and Kim and I would put our hands through the middle of the sheets to keep them warm.

We moved again and settled in Kent Village, Maryland. I went to a little school up on a hill. I was in the fourth grade. I made a friend named Joyce that year who was to remain my best friend for many years. She is the godmother to my daughter. In fact, I adopted her parents as my own. I was an extremely unhappy child then. Momma Betty had arms to hold and soothe me. Joyce and I were like sisters. We played in the common playground. We were always with each other doing something. We lived not so far from each other. I confided all my deepest secrets to her. We knew everything about each other. She was my Maid of Honour at my wedding and I played the same role at hers.

I have lost touch with Joyce. I would love her to see pictures of Stacey's children and catch up with her. She was such an important part of my life and a safe port in the many storms that occurred then. When looking back at us I would say she was a mirror for me to see my goodness. We did not have things in common; we had opposites to experience. She certainly brought out the best in me when we were together. She was the person I turned to whenever my mom was drunk, I had been beaten and when I was raped. Again, I did not tell my parents, I was too ashamed. I developed a pattern of having only one close friend. I did not trust very many people. I clung on to Joyce as I would eventually cling to all my friends until Reiki came into my life. Yes, I had other friends, but they were more surface relationship ones, kids to play with but not share my feelings.

We had moved again when I started High School, so I went through similar feelings of being on the outside looking in. However, I met my first love, Phil, and my best friend, Lin, at High School. My daughter Stacey's middle name is Lin, after my friend. We are still in touch. She and her husband are now grandparents and we laugh at our times in High School. Phil and I write at Christmas. Lasting friendship shared across the miles. I was very much a loner. I had a few close friends and many acquaintances. Because of the problems at home I rarely brought anyone there. I spent what time I had available with my friends at their houses. I needed to feel secure and relaxed. I did not have this at home. So my friends became people with whom I could be myself and accepted. Certainly, it was not all bleak. I worked, went to school and had a good time with a few people. Looking back now from this perspective, I see how lonely I was and that what I was looking for outside myself I received from my friends. They were the ones whom I felt complete with. The journey inward and the completeness I now feel would come later and with other friends.

Our need for friends and what their friendship brings is different throughout the stages of our life. In infant school it can be the need for a playmate. In primary and secondary school there is a social interaction. We have friends in the various clubs we belong to or the activities we do. We have friends whom we confide in and we befriend the opposite sex, who are either the people with whom we hang around or become closer to us. So they fulfil different functions in our life. Some remain in our lives and some go. Each leaves a thread in the tapestry we weave of our lives.

I always thought it was so neat that kids in High School would tease each other about things that had happened when they were in first grade. They had a history with each other that was built on many experiences. I envied them the longevity of friendship. They envied me because I had travelled so much. The grass is truly greener on the other side of the fence. Both experiences certainly give you something. For me, it has been easier to move and change. I developed a 'my home is where I hang my hat' type of attitude, whereas my former classmates may have problems being uprooted. When I

REIKI FOR THE SOUL

catch up with them, I find that they have longer lasting friendships.

When we move into adult relationships we often find that our friends share our beliefs. We can be in agreement with them about many things such as religion, politics, work, play and so on. If we are interested in sports, our friends will typically be people with whom we will go to a game or watch it on television. Mothers get to know each other through the friendships made by their children. At college, we make social friends who may continue to play an important part in our lives, especially as we move into a work environment and begin making a name for ourselves.

We will have many acquaintances, some of whom we will call friends. When I was divorced I made friends with some other divorced women. What we had in common was that we were single mothers and most of our daughters were friends in school. One friend in particular, Judy, and I spent a lot of time together. We had both been through a bad marriage, so we had an agreement about how men are. We would get together after work for a drink and talk about men. There were also times when other divorced women would get together with us and, of course, the topic was very often men and the problems we were experiencing as single mothers. Each one of us had a more traumatic story to tell. We were a very sympathetic audience. Certainly there were shoulders to cry on, a place to be with each other and to be understood. What was constant was that we were not encouraging each other to have a different belief system. We, in fact, encouraged each other to keep it. If we believed men were bad, then we would be attracting bad men into our lives. I am getting ahead in the story.

One Thanksgiving, Judy's family, Stacey, and I had dinner together. It was a joint effort of making a dinner and having a wonderful atmosphere. Her brother Jon and his wife had just completed a course that they said was life-changing. It was called the 'Life Training'. They suggested we do it to help us live our lives differently. Judy was given the course as an early Christmas present and I decided to treat myself. Not only that, I enrolled my mother into the training as well. We went and I had my first experience of transformational training. It was to be one of the biggest steps I was to take to come back to a peace of mind. Coupled with Reiki, they have been instrumental in the changes that continue to occur. My mother and I fell into each other's arms at the end of the weekend. It was a big opening for us. Judy made such movement in her personal life. Things were never to be the same.

I noticed that the women who did not take the training with us stayed stuck where they were. When we got together I did not want to talk about men being bad; I was willing to see and experience that not all men are bad. Much more, I had decided I had been responsible for creating my life and wanted to create something different. We didn't seem to have anything in common any more. I had changed and they had not. They were uncomfortable with me because I did not believe as they did. I was challenging them to feel and think differently. I was uncomfortable with them because we didn't have as much in common. Those friends after a while seemed to fall away.

What came in their place were many more people who had been through an awakening experience and were actively working on themselves. It was exciting to be with each other. We were supporting each other emotionally, mentally and spiritually. Life took on new meaning with these friends.

I have not lived in the United States for 10 years. At the beginning of this year I spent a lovely evening with 10 of my Life Training buddies as we caught up with each other's lives, and found out what had happened since the last time we were together. We have been friends for almost 20 years; they are deep and rewarding friendships. We continue to support each other, to celebrate our achievements, to uphold our spirits. I feel like I have my own cheering squad.

The same thing holds true in our family of Reiki. I have many friends and friendships with the students I have taught Reiki to. The context for my Association is one of brotherhood and family. The friendships I have made within the Reiki community all over the world are beautiful. We have a group of Masters that correspond with each other, sharing information, insight and ideas. We send energy to each other. Many of us live so far away from each other, we nearly transverse the globe. We come from different schools of Reiki, some more traditional than others. What we have in common is a love for Reiki, and we have a deep sense of being in the centre of the practice. In this centre is love. These friendships are precious. They are built on a commonality and yet we acknowledge and love the differences we each bring to each other. We share our joy and sadness and we celebrate each other. Life is so rich with these people in my life.

When I was little my mom told me I would be lucky if I had five friends in my life. She said a true friend would clean up after you if you were sick and stay beside you when you gave birth to your children and when you died. I have found some truth in this from my own experience.

A couple of years ago I had to have emergency surgery on my knee as I had ruptured the meniscus. Danny, my assistant, was helping me once I came home from the hospital. He would come every day in the morning to dress me and fix some food and in the evening to put me to bed. One day I was so desperate for a shower I asked him if there was a way I could get wet. He got me undressed and managed to put my leg in the orthopaedic brace on the toilet and the rest of me leaning into the tub. The shower was so wonderful. I said to him, 'I bet when you came to work for me you never thought you would be giving me a bath.' He replied, 'No, I didn't. However, I am your friend and that is what friends are for.' It was a very touching moment for me. I was so exposed, helpless and yet knew I was loved and taken care of. Danny at that time was 24 years old. He and his wife are still dear friends.

To say the quality of my life and the depth of my friendships have changed as I have integrated Reiki into my life would be understated. I feel as if I am finally living and embracing life with the friends I have. It is not the quantity of friends one has but the quality of friendship we can bring to each other. What then is reflected back to me when I am with these wonderful people is light and love. I am truly blessed!

Grandmother says:

Friendships are like jewels. You can spend a lifetime looking at the many facets of one jewel. You can either be on the surface of it or allow yourself to experience the depth. When it is dirty you can wash it. You can either put it away in a vault because you think it too precious to share or share its beauty with all that come near. Too many jewels are treated like casual friends; they are acquired to make you look like more than you are, and often worn to bring you praise. How you treat a friend will be how you are treated. If you are only interested in being one of many without real appreciation then you will go for quantity. But, if you go for quality and depth, you will be blessed many times over. A true friend will take the time to see and appreciate your every flaw and attribute. A friend will love you for your vibrancy as well as the times you do not shine so brightly.

What do you remember about your friendships that were formed in infant school?

_____

_____

_____

_____

Who was your best friend and why? What did you have in common?

_____

_____

_____

_____

In primary and secondary school, what types of friends did you have?

_____

_____

_____

_____

How were friendships formed in your later years, such as at university or college? And what purpose did they serve?

_____

_____

_____

_____

How about friendships now. Have you noticed a different quality to them, and if so what?

_____

_____

_____

_____

Who is your oldest friend, not in age but in length of time? What is their gift to you and have you acknowledged them lately for it?

_____

_____

_____

_____

Do you have a friend who is no longer in your life but you wish was? If they are living, will you contact them?

_____

_____

_____

_____

Can you be your own best friend, and if so, what does that look like?

_____

_____

_____

_____

Are you a good friend and why?

_____

_____

_____

_____

After answering the questions, take time to sit quietly and feel your body. Remember that revisiting areas of your life may also bring up emotions that you may not have expressed in a long time. Take the time to give yourself a self-treatment. By loving into yourself you set these emotions free and acknowledge the importance of each step you have taken.

Close your eyes and take a deep, cleansing breath. Feel your body. Are there areas that are tight or heavy? Are there places in you that need to be touched and loved into? Use your hands to touch these places. Give yourself Reiki to return these areas into harmony. If you have been initiated into Reiki two energy, use the power and emotional mental symbols to work deeply to return yourself to a state of inner harmony and peace.

Honour yourself and your journey thus far.

霊

気

THE DOORWAY OF
RELATIONSHIPS

WE may think that being in a relationship is also about being in love. This is an aspect of having a relationship, but we are in relationship with all things, every being that is in our world, including ourselves. Some relationships are closer than others; and sometimes we don't even realize we are in a relationship with someone at all. In all cases these relationships provide the true motivation and the vehicle for completing our personal purpose, which is to be happy. As simple as it sounds, the truest purpose of our life is happiness. When we are unhappy, our personal healing becomes our first priority. When we are in a loving relationship with all things, we then experience fulfilment. Relationships do not fulfil us – only we can do that. I think of happiness as returning to the centre of my being, home in my heart and soul, resting in the light of all there is and a oneness. This is an experience that is free from ego and the need to define myself. My happiness is not dependent on someone providing it for me; it comes from the inside and radiates outward.

Relationships support us to heal ourselves as we move through life. The wounds from our past are exposed in order for our continued growth to be possible. We relive our past through our relationships. The patterns of the tapestry we wove before are re-examined, and only through healing past heartache can we move forward to weave a finer pattern in the future. This is done through love, communication and forgiveness.

In the summer of '94 I went with a group of Czech friends to an island off the coast of Yugoslavia named Rab. We spent 10 days there in the sun at a resort. I arranged for a little water taxi to take me each morning to a secluded part of the island where I could sunbathe and do some writing, and to pick me up in the evening at sunset. I had been in a period of deep searching and had the intention of just allowing myself to be sourced by relaxing and being quiet. The following are excerpts from my diary during that time and my thoughts about what I discovered.

AUGUST SECOND

The point of understanding

God loves us so much that he/she continues to give us opportunities to find our way home. Home is the place where we experience our spiritual truth and divinity. These opportunities come in the form of choice. Choose to respond into the world or to react. The reaction becomes the instrument that separates us from the source in all things. Because we are truly one, this separateness is then a fracturing of the whole. Most of the time we are unaware of our responses or reactions because we are asleep.

Our journey is one of reawakening to the source within us and then to see this source in all things. This will bring us into a relationship with ourselves through that which exists outside of the Ego State. We truly have the capacity to be one with all things by recognizing and responding to the sameness in everything. This sameness is 'The Light'. All other than light is an illusion, and a mask worn from conditioning. Our reactions thus become fixed on our faces and bodies and keep us separated from each other.

The American Indians say that our 'awake' time is the illusion. We see through eyes that filter information through the brain that has been filled with our reactionary patterns and our very good reasons for believing them to be true. We are for the most part unable to make clear choices because of our programmed mind. Our reasoning gets in the way of us seeing clearly.

Our hearts also respond and react to vibration. All choices carry a vibrational quality that we will feel in our body. We have a developed knowing inside of us to also feel if the choices we make will support us spiritually.

The American Indians also say that our 'sleep' time is our reality. We have let go of our preconceptions and have returned to the state of unlimited expression of love and oneness. It is during this time we are rejoined to our spiritual truth. We fly like eagles back home expressing ourselves as one and as God. We are not separated from God as he is the source and so are we. All else is illusion. God is in dwelling in us. As we strip away illusion in order to respond rather than react, the more we lose the 'I' of man and can experience the source within us. In this stage there is simply more room for God to be there and to work through us. As we empty the vessel of illusion it is instantly filled with truth, 'The Light'.

The point of understanding comes when we no longer see ourselves as a vessel to be emptied or refilled. We experience ourselves as one with all things. We have become one with the rocks, trees, birds, insects, air, water and all people. When we treat all things as God we move into a concert of life, we are the music and the composer. Therefore the truth is the oneness. We are in God and God is in us. This is the finest expression of relationship.

AUGUST THIRD

Finding perfection

I had a specific map about perfection and the perfect relationship. My map contained all the information I needed to judge the correctness of things, and of course I knew what perfection and a perfect relationship looked like and what must be done to have them. My mind could see the things necessary and in an instant find the things that did not add up to perfection. Obtaining perfection in myself and in relationship is a hard task, as I never will really achieve it. There is always something moving or changing. Just when I think I have it, my goal manages to slip through my fingers one more time.

One day I realized I had lost my map. How imperfect of me! At first I panicked. My mind said I would never reach perfection or have that perfect relationship because I had no directions as to how to get to these things. I wouldn't know how to be. I sat quietly looking through my mind for where I had misplaced it. I was retracing my steps of the past several days.

I saw myself sitting on a rock in my special place. I was looking out to sea and the gulls were flying. The light was like magic on the water, making reflections of many colours. I was connected to all things, one with the world and all in it. I could hear myself say, 'Life is perfect, as it is nothing ever needs to be changed.' At that point my map was lost. However, I had been found at the same time as I moved into a beautiful relationship with my world.

AUGUST FOURTH

How will I know?

How will I know I'm fully awakened?
You will cease to ask or to look for what needs to happen to experience oneness.

Seasons
When I was little I always felt that the sunshine was God's kiss.
Now I realize his kisses in all the seasons.

A talk with God
I want to look into your eyes, father.
You do in each moment you see anything.
I want to be embraced by you, father.
You are. For as you allow others to touch and hold you, you in turn hold others. It is all the same, for all are I.
I want to teach about awakening, father.
Then stand forth awakened and others will join you. Teaching is not giving information, rather living the principle of what you teach. Be the example. Be awake.
What is my purpose, father?
You are living your purpose in every moment, you are on your way home.

AUGUST FIFTH

Goals

I don't know why I resist so much. When I am in the flow things happen to support the vision held in my heart of an awakened and peace-filled world. But then something happens that seems to test me. Things slow down and even stop. I become afraid. Is the fear created then? Or is the fear really there all along and is what stops the momentum?
What am I afraid of? Is it that I won't reach the goal?
Or perhaps the goal will be realized, and if so, what then?

AUGUST SIXTH

I am so busy trying to lose myself, yet I keep finding myself in everyone I see!
Perhaps it is not to see the conditioned masks that fear has put into place,
Rather to see the light of God that is there.
For who am I?
Is it the illusion called man or the Light which is God?

AUGUST SEVENTH

Where God lives

When I was little I remember saying, 'God doesn't live in this church.' People were ashamed of me for saying that. I didn't understand why because I found God alive in the flowers, trees, birds, rocks and my playmates. He spoke to me through these things. I am glad I didn't understand their God and knew mine.

AUGUST EIGHTH

The witness

Being a witness to someone's transformational process is transforming in itself. As we are truly one. When one aspect of the whole is transformed, the other parts transform as well. It calls forth in us a relationship to the very vibrational qualities we witness.

AUGUST NINTH

Today

Today is perfect; I do things at my own pace, which is surprisingly not fast. The many things my mind normally says must be done do not drive me. I have listened to my breath, felt a gentle breeze on my skin, enjoyed the feeling of the water moving through my fingers. I have read, written the messages I continue to receive. I am not bored at all; the fact is I am more alive than I have been before. Nothing depends on me, not even myself. I am part of everything and yet nothing. Every cell is alive. I feel everything, yet keep nothing except the memory of this time. Surely this is enlightenment.

AUGUST TENTH

Sandcastles

Today there are many sandcastles on the beach built by a diversity of people. Each has a unique shape. Some look like a fortress, strong and foreboding; another looks like a fairy princess could live there, it is pretty, open and inviting. There is but one thing they have in common. They are not permanent. They took a long time to build, gave an immense amount of pleasure and by tomorrow they will be gone, washed away with the tide. Could this be like human beings?

AUGUST ELEVENTH

Last week versus this week

Last week there was a rhythm to the day. The water was low in the morning and high in the afternoon. The water refrigerator was first on the right and then on the left side of the lagoon as the sun and tide changed its direction. The towels dried better on the yew tree. Today the rhythm has changed. It is as if all is backwards or upside down. I was tired this morning and there was more water then. I am better this afternoon and there is less water. Is this a phase of the moon or is it my perception that is different? How strange it is to feel these differences in my body, my whole being. I liked last week better; it felt more whole. Even subtle changes give us choices.

AUGUST TWELFTH

Harmony

As I sit and look out of the window of the bus taking me back to the Czech Republic I am struck by how everything has its own rhythm. Every aspect of a human being has its own music or vibration. When the aspects of the body are in harmony it is as if they are playing beautiful music together. If something is out of balance, then it is like the instrument is playing out of tune. When the body's vibration is not in tune then the music does not sound as pretty. In fact, listening could be a terrible experience. The same holds true with groups of people who come together. If each person in the group is in harmony then the result is an orchestra creating a beautiful symphony. I imagine God is the conductor.

Today

Reading through the messages I had been given over those 10 days I realized that all of the messages or realizations had something to do with relationships. With every message came opportunity and choice. I had been brought to the point of choosing to relate or not to God, nature, others, myself and to oneness. Each day my sensitivity was increased so much that I felt the slightest changes in my surroundings, because I was the surroundings. I was one with all things and sourced beyond measure. It has been a profound lesson for me to experience my relationship to all things on so many levels. I have also realized that when I am with people and I am in harmony I can feel if they are in harmony or not. I can hear the music as we come together. I send them second-degree Reiki energy when I feel a 'sour note' so that they can heal themselves and come back into tune.

Everything is so interdependent. Once you have given yourself this gift there will never be any doubt of these inter-relationships. I gaze at the stars at night, feel their energy, and know that this connection also extends out past this world to the universe and what lies beyond. How I treat Mother Earth is also an indication of how I treat myself. If I am concerned about her and how she has become contaminated I must also be concerned enough to see how I have polluted myself with thoughts, emotions and food that have become toxic in my body, mind and spirit. One of the most beautiful aspects about Reiki is the experience of returning to an inner and peaceful core. As more of us make this return we will also see a change in our environment. Instead of making war with each other we can then work together to make environmental changes. We are naturally more 'response-able' to our world. The work always starts within and radiates outward. The journey home is then a profound one because its effects are experienced on a global level.

When I was younger, before Reiki, I had no idea about responsibility. I felt it was a heavy task. Something that others placed on your shoulders to carry. After all, I had been responsible for my mother and my brother for most of my life. I certainly felt I was responsible for the men who abused me when I was little, and for my daughter's kidnapping. I would take responsibility on willingly as a way to prove I was not such a bad girl after all. Someone has to do it, why not me?

When I did the Life Training I remember Ann McMasters standing in front of the room and defining responsibility. I had such a realization that I could come into a different relationship with a word and all it implied. She said, 'Responsibility is the ability to respond in the moment with love.' When we are reaction-free we are able to do this. Reaction is not love, it is the reverse.

With regards to having relationships with others, all relationships bring us the opportunity to see ourselves mirrored in each other. My memories are so full of people who have made lasting impressions in my life. The gifts they have brought to me by showing me myself have helped me come into harmony, even if I experienced pain at the time. Chipping away at the ego is always painful.

A Spiritual Teacher

I was asked to teach Reiki in a spiritual centre in Poland. Andrej is the head of the centre there and a renowned healer throughout Eastern Europe. He wrote asking me to come and teach Reiki to him, his students and some of his critically ill patients.

I had no idea what to expect the day I arrived at his centre. I had never been to Poland. I was shown into his study. There was no translator with us. Andrej looked intently into my eyes and we became connected. There was such an incredible energy between us. I heard him talking to me and understood him without a problem. The only thing was he was not physically speaking. I was told to relax, not to be afraid, as fear would separate us. Andrej told me that he had seen me in a dream. He went on to say that we would be teaching each other important things that would help with our work. He assured me that I was still on the ground and again not to be afraid. He was delighted that I could hear him this way.

That was my first experience with telepathic communication. Over the course of 10 days I worked with him every evening and taught Reiki classes during the day. Each evening brought new challenges. It seemed to me that we were working on different levels. Andrej told me I was not permitted to ask questions. I was to write them down and I would have my answers by the end of the week. Andrej taught me to heal with the mind, to direct energy, to work on the different levels of the client's energy field, to work with the denseness of thought and emotion, and to do psychic surgery.

When we finished our clinical practice at night there were discussions with his students and patients who would give feedback about their experiences of the work I was doing with them and what they felt and/or saw. Finally, in the last moments of night I would write all my questions in my book. I had so much that I needed an explanation for. I was fascinated and felt as if I was reaching a new depth to my work with people. I could see how Reiki and mind-directed energy could be combined to create another energy. It was like a marriage of the heart and the mind. When I looked at the energy it was like a braid made from silver and gold, yet contained within were all the colours of the rainbow as well. I also saw Reiki energy and felt it coming into me.

Andrej explained that in natural healing each healer worked with a certain vibrational quality. This vibration or oscillation had a colour and sound associated with it. Their particular vibration worked better to cure specific illnesses. One of the reasons he had several healers working with one person was that the patient needed those colours for their healing. He told me that the healers needed to be able to move into harmony and the changes necessary for this involved their ego. Some of the healers were not happy being perhaps the red vibration and thought another colour might be better. Or they had lost sight of the necessity to work as a whole bouquet of colour. Andrej felt Reiki would help them to be more heart-centred and come from an inner core that involved love.

I wondered why Andrej worked alone and not with the others, and why he didn't ask me to work with anyone. He smiled and, looking deeply into my eyes, said, 'You work with all the vibrations. The over-arching colours are silver and gold, yet within this spectrum is all there is and more.' Andrej went on to say, 'I know I am, the problem is you do not know.' I said to him, 'When will I know?' 'Soon,' he replied.

I awoke on the Saturday morning feeling a bit hungover. I had not had anything to drink. I guessed there was so much I was attempting to integrate that my body was tired of trying to fit 'it' all in place. I wanted to pull the covers over my head and sleep more, especially since there were no Reiki classes today. Just as I had decided to do just that, Andrej knocked on my door and told me I would be going to visit some sacred sights during the day and that in the evening I would have a spiritual initiation.

He laughed as I tried to focus on his telepathic communication and pointed to a woman standing nearby in the hallway. She introduced herself as Magda and said that Andrej thought I needed a break from concentration and she would act as my translator during this special day. I hurriedly dressed. When I arrived at the car, Andrej was not there. I was told he would see me that night and all my questions would be answered. He remembered!

I was taken to a basilica and saw a pile of crutches by the door. I asked why they were there and was told the people who had prayed for a miracle and could walk afterwards left them. The energy was so sweet in the entire place. Next we went to a waterfall that was a place of pilgrimage. Again I was told that miraculous cures happened there. At all the places we visited that day we would kneel down and ask for God's love and blessing. I always heard them asking for a miracle for me. I began to feel that the initiation was something so special that I wanted to come to it pure. I asked if I could buy a white scarf to cover my head that evening. The people with me smiled and handed me a package. When I opened it, there was a white scarf inside. They had anticipated my wishes.

Andrej met the car as we returned and said to get ready for the timing was just about right. I went to my room and took a shower and washed my hair. I slipped on a simple dress. I wore no make-up or jewellery, just the white scarf over my head, and walked to the place he had picked for this initiation. Andrej sat me in a chair facing a beautiful altar. On the altar were a white candle, a white rose and a picture of Christ. He instructed me to close my eyes and I did.

The hour of my initiation was 9 p.m. I do not remember anything other than his hands touching my head and an incredible light entering into me. It seemed as if I disappeared. When I was aware of myself in the room, I was alone, yet I started having such beautiful experiences. I looked at the rose and became the rose. I was the scent, the petal, and the stamen. I became the candle and the candle flame. I experienced the difference in the intensity of the colour of the flame. I went into the picture of Christ and became Christ and my heart burst in compassion. I could feel coloured lights coming from my heart. I looked at the rocking chair and became the runner of the chair. I could feel the wood compress as the chair rocked. Whatever I would think of I became. A glass of water, the glass that held it, all was in my experience. A drop of moisture and the air, all were in my ability to feel and express. I could smell everything, hear everything, I was everything.

Andrej entered the room and touched me on the shoulder softly. He said to come with him, that the students were waiting. I sat down in another room and looked at the clock. It was midnight. The people were so alive in the room and filled with grace. Andrej asked me, 'What were those questions you wanted to ask?' I looked at him and smiled saying, 'I have no questions for I know.' 'What do you know my sister?' was his question. I took a breath and said, 'I am God.'

This beautiful state of bliss lasted 21 days. In those precious days I had such clarity, humility, compassion and peace. I ate no food; I only drank fresh water that Andrej energized with his hands. I was in the centre of the universe; there certainly were no questions to ask and no experiences to feel. I moved through the day as if I was floating. All I had to do was think and I was there. During that time I travelled and worked with so many people. I worked on levels of the earth and beyond, yet my body never moved from the chair I was sitting in.

Afterwards I asked Andrej what I could possibly gift him with for the blessing of oneness. He told me I had given him far more than I could realize. He said he had been feeling so alone in his work. Andrej felt that he was only understood at some level. Being with me was having family that felt and thought the same way as he did. I knew what he was saying as I had felt this too. He went on to say, 'I can see the cells in the body, see how the bones mend if broken. I can take illness from a person and they call it a miracle. But until you taught me Reiki I only used my head. Now I see the whole person I am working on and I have compassion for them. I have been brought into a relationship with love. You see, I feel I have received the bigger blessing during this time we have been together.'

A few years later I wondered just what had happened to me that time I was in Poland with Andrej. I decided to sit quietly and just ask for an explanation. This is what I heard:

The soul is born into man and it is man's point of reference to his unity with God the father and the mother. As man progresses, the point of reference can seem to be further away. However, it is deep inside man and will act as a homing beacon when it has been activated. The vibration of this point of light, the soul, is always constant and is the light. Often times this light is encapsulated by the denseness of reaction, or if the body is too dense it will force the soul light to exit the body by some degree. This light that has left the physical body stays around the individual waiting for a moment to incarnate again.

The matter of man is dense. Matter comprises all reaction. Therefore the light of the soul may not be seen as light for it is cloaked. It is seen and reborn in an initiation. This is considered an awakening moment. All awakenings are as different as man is different. Yet this awakening serves as a point of reference that the soul has entered into a new relationship with the body. The homing beacon that is now reawakened will serve to remind the person their way home is through the compassion of the heart.

Spirit and physical work together in man. This physical journey with the soul involves an inner and outer experience. The physically awakened man then progresses, as the soul guides the journey and the depth of experience.

In your case it was the experience of death and rebirth. In this rebirth rose forth a unity. This has become your point of reference. For the past 25 years your journey has been in the inner world, experiencing the darkness and the outer world, being in the light. You have understood the concept with a rational mind. Your experience has been to experience polarity. You have been letting go of your ego and your need to be separate, you have been asking for and giving forgiveness. All this has been in preparation for your time with Andrej.

The initiation with Andrej has been the awakening of Divine spirit. 'I am the light' is not just a concept. It is your reality. You know because you have experienced yourself so. The soul of man has a direct experience of joining with God. Usually people only experience this when they drop their physical bodies as it is a death of matter and the need to hold on to the physical body. This death of matter is not just a physical death, as we know it; rather this matter changes into other energy. Be not afraid. Fear breeds density. When you have no fear you are unified. You are the 'I' am and the 'I' am the light that sources all. In this state you knew there was no time, no beginning or end. You were everywhere and everything. You were God. In fact, you still are, only aspects of you have forgotten. It is much safer to play life small, but being small does not call others out to their own majesty. When will you remember? We hope soon for there is much to be done.

What do you feel is the hardest part about being in relationship with yourself?

_____

_____

_____

_____

What has been your biggest challenge to be in relationship with others? Describe how you have overcome this.

_____

_____

_____

_____

Are you in relationship with nature, animals and our world? If so, what does this look like to you? How does it feel in your body?

_____

_____

_____

_____

What turning points in your life have helped to awaken you to your divinity and to your relationship to oneness?

_____

_____

_____

_____

Who has been instrumental in your relationship to 'all there is'?

_____

_____

_____

_____

After answering the questions, take time to sit quietly and feel your body. Remember that revisiting areas of your life may also bring up emotions that you may not have expressed in a long time. Take the time to give yourself a self-treatment. By loving into yourself you set these emotions free and acknowledge the importance of each step you have taken.

Close your eyes and take a deep, cleansing breath. Feel your body. Are there areas that are tight or heavy? Are there places in you that need to be touched and loved into? Use your hands to touch these places. Give yourself Reiki to return these areas into harmony. If you have been initiated into Reiki two energy, use the power and emotional mental symbols to work deeply to return yourself to a state of inner harmony and peace.

Honour yourself and your journey thus far.

霊
気

THE DOORWAY
OF LOVE

I STOOD at the doorway holding the doorknob in my hand, listening to my mind busily trying to convince me that going in here was not a good idea … This door was better left alone. It had been a long time since you visited this place and there could be bad things just behind the door. I knew that I had been to this space many times, but perhaps I was unfamiliar with some of the streets and it was time to do some exploring. Certainly opening a door marked love was sure to bring me many revelations … I took a breath, pushed the door open and walked inside.

Welcome! You certainly struggled with your mind for a while. I have enjoyed watching your progress and can say you have enough love for yourself to have at least entered into this space and a willingness to explore. That is to be commended. Do you know what you may find here? What are you hoping to experience?

Grandmother, I had a feeling that I would find you here. It is nice knowing that at every moment you are there for me. You love me enough to challenge me to be real. I have no idea what is here. I am hoping that I will find that the work I have done regarding love will indicate that I have more understanding of love than my mind says I do.

So are you saying love is a challenge, and that you can only be real if you are challenged to be so?

Well, I wasn't thinking it was a challenge or that I had to be challenged to be real. I thought that part of the way you loved me and all of us who listen to you was to challenge our beliefs so that we could see if they were true or not. When we made choices we could then be more real.

But, my dear child, all of your beliefs are true. What I do with you, perhaps, is to challenge their validity and ask of you to feel if the belief you have supports you into your lightness or your darkness. As you come closer to your inner core and to the light, all that is darkness or reaction has an opportunity to be healed. In this healing process beliefs that you have held as true for so long are tested. Hopefully those beliefs that keep you from your truest divinity will be discarded. There is no demand when and if this happens, for you are in charge of your destiny. You are always the creative essence and have freewill choice. I will keep asking you if what you are creating will promote a feeling of 'good' to you. As you know, for all your actions, there will be a response or a reaction. That is cause and effect at play or Karma. How real do you wish to be and what is real to you?

Real, well that is a question. I would imagine now that you have asked me if I have held real as being my divinity and not being real as being anything else. Now, as I say this, I also see that I have been quite black and white about this word. Either I am or I am not real. There is no grey space.

Exactly! That is old stuff concerning your need to be perfect and that essentially keeps you from your divinity as it is all separating thoughts. If you, for instance, say I must be real, you are therefore saying you are not. That what you are is an illusion. Since you are indeed the creative aspect in your life, how can you create if you are an illusion of yourself? And if you could create as this illusion, wouldn't you just create more illusion?

Your words and thoughts are such powerful instruments. Yet not many people will realize that in all moments they have created themselves out of this dynamic. It is far too easy to blame others for this and not take responsibility. Therefore I ask you, have you created thoughts and feelings about love that are supporting you to be in your majesty and grace or in your darkness? Take a few moments to let this question sink in. Feel with your whole being where the ideas of love reside in you in this moment.

I heard her question echoing in my ears, 'Have you created thoughts and feelings about love that are supporting you to be in your majesty and grace or in your darkness?' That is certainly the question. Now to explore what is here. Perhaps I will find what exactly what these thoughts and feelings may be.

Love Hurts

When I was a little girl I was afraid of the water. I would sit by it and feel safe, but to be in it was a torture, especially to have my head pushed under the water. I did not have any recall of why I was afraid. I just was. When we lived in Tripoli my dad and his friend decided it was time to teach me to swim. It was an idea I was not keen on. I had been in the pool but held on to the edge. I would not let go and was terribly scared if I couldn't touch the bottom. Dad picked me up that hot afternoon and threw me right in the centre of the pool. I went down three times and then gathered the strength needed to dog-paddle to the edge. I was so upset about being thrown in, but most of all I was hurt because they thought it was so funny. I decided that love hurt. Most of all, parents hurt their children and thought it was funny.

Many years later when I was in therapy I was talking about my fear of water when I was little. The therapist asked me what the fear felt like and I explained that I could not breathe. Using some techniques she worked with me to discover why my fear of water was tied to my breath. I recalled a moment when I was about a month old when my mom was giving me a bath in the sink. I was crying and wouldn't stop. She forced my face under the water. I took that as she was trying to kill me. All sorts of beliefs were put into place at that young age. Love hurts, I can't trust my mom, I am bad because things like this do not happen to good girls (babies). I was astounded that I remembered this so clearly that I even had problems breathing as I talked about what had happened to the therapist.

The next step was to verify if this had happened and why. I went to my mother and told her I'd had an interesting session with the therapist and had remembered something that did not seem possible. I asked her if she ever held my face under the water when I was a baby. She looked at me with big eyes and said, 'Oh my goodness, you were just a small girl then, I guess about six weeks old. I had started to bathe you and you just began crying. I did not know what to do with you and felt so inadequate as a mother. No one had given me a clue what to do when a baby cries and will not stop. So I decided to put your face under the water to shock you and perhaps you would stop crying.' I asked her, 'Did it work?' She replied, 'Yes, but you always had a problem with being in the water since then.'

I told her about the decisions I had made about her and myself because of that experience. I also told her that she was doing the best she could then, as I knew I didn't come with an instruction book. Then I asked her to forgive me for thinking that I could not trust her and that she would always hurt me, as she loved me. Fortunately, we both had done the Life Training and had the tools to clear our minds. I realized through this experience that I had a belief structure in place when I was four to six weeks old about how love is, and when I was eight years old my mind had said the same thing again in regards to my dad throwing me in the pool. At that time I was reinforcing my belief system. My belief was so strong; I attracted the very thing I feared the most to happen to me. I also got to be right about love hurting, one more time. This was a pattern that would be a main theme in my life for a long while. It was such a moment of freedom when she forgave me. I had been holding that against her for many years without really knowing why. I just knew I didn't trust her and that in some way she would hurt me. Now we could create from a different place with each other.

What early decisions did you make about love? Can you remember why they were made? Are these decisions supporting you into your light or darkness?

_____

_____

_____

_____

Are you still holding on to resentment and judgement about someone in your life, for all your very good reasons? Is there another way to see the situation, forgive and let love in?

REIKI FOR THE SOUL

_____
_____
_____
_____

In this moment, how much lightness and darkness have you created in you concerning love?

_____
_____
_____
_____

Trusting Love? No, Not at this Moment

I sat in a chair that just happened to be in the room looking at the boxes that were stacked for the move. They represented the lifetime of our relationship, all the things we both thought were important, and yet I realized at this moment they were not. I had systematically gone through every cabinet and closet, dividing spoons, knives and forks, half for him and half for us. The table would go and the chairs would remain. I had purchased another antique one to take its place. Towels we had shared were now divided. He liked the green ones and I kept the ones in rose. Last night was the worst night. I sorted the photos. The first part was easy – he got his family pictures and I got mine. I struggled with wanting to keep his photo and in the end I did not. Love was too painful right now.

We had been so civil about the separation, making up lists of things we wanted and reaching a compromise on the rest. I imagine I was a typical woman who wanted the radio and did not realize that that was what worked the rest of the system. He got ours and he bought me a smaller version. We had two televisions so that was no problem.

Our taste in music was about the same so we split those down the middle. Each room was sorted and packed. Some of the things we hadn't used in years. It became a good excuse to let things go. The Christmas decorations were harder. In the end Stacey chose what she wanted, and we halved the rest. There were the moments of sadness when I thought as I held a toy soldier we purchased that when …

The things in the garage were no difficulty. I needed the lawnmower and he took the tools. It was funny how some of the rooms were more his and others more mine. How did we manage to accumulate so much and learn so little about love?

We had two couches; he left those for us. He took the office furniture and I kept the bedroom, yet little did I realize that for months after this I wouldn't be able to sleep in the bed. I moved mechanically through the house waiting for his moving van to appear. I had finished questioning the rightness of it all. I had numbed myself out so feeling wasn't a question. I wanted this to end and get on with my life.

I had decided to stay in the house for Stacey's stability. I hadn't thought how hard it would be for me to live in the house. I wanted Ken to be comfortable in his new situation; I had not considered what my comfort looked like. I struggled to keep myself together so that when he walked into the house he would feel it was the right decision. Strong to the end was my motto. How I wished I could let the scared Mari out. I had trusted him more than any other person. What did I do now with this emptiness inside me? Was there a way to move back into trust and to trusting love? First, I had to make it through this night.

Stacey was so angry; she didn't understand how the man she called daddy was walking out of her life. She blamed me for not doing and being enough to keep it all together. I wished I could tell her it would get better, but I didn't want to lie. I found it hard to be a mother in these moments; I just wanted to be a wife. I would certainly have settled for being a little girl so I wouldn't have to worry about tomorrow or the next day.

My mind was active as I looked out the window. It was playing the 'what if' game. Ah! the endless scenarios it dreamed up. I ran these same thoughts through my mind for days since he left in the darkness of night. I couldn't get the words out I thought he needed to hear. The only thing that came to mind is *come see us sometime*. I would have liked to have told him how much he meant to me all these years, but my mind said the words will just fall on deaf ears, best to keep quiet and not make a scene. How did I trust love would be different the second time around?

When he left, his best friend Jim called and said that Ken wasn't mine to keep. I needed to open my hand and let him fly free. I remember thinking I understand that about birds, but this is different because he is part of my heart. He had completed me. We were like two dolphins swimming in the sea. We were dependent on each other. Now I had to learn to stand on two feet even though I only had one.

The truck arrived. I wanted to run away and hide. I heard these words coming from deep in my heart, 'This is a grown up game and I want no part of it.' Another aspect of Mari speaking her mind. Dear God, what did I do right? It seems as if everything had gone wrong. How could I have been so silly to have trusted love this time? My mind has always known how things would work out.

The door closed on the van and it pulled away. I managed just to keep myself together with no tears. Stacey was not home as it was too hard for her to face the finality of it all. Something more to deal with later when she did come home. The final words when we parted came painfully slow. 'When I get settled come and see me.' I said, 'Maybe so.'

This happened 17 years ago. I did close down and decide that once again love was painful and not to be trusted. I spent time finding my other leg and learning to stand on both of my feet. After three years or so I finally got angry. Angry with Ken for leaving and angry with myself for taking all the blame. The hard crust was finally breaking down so that the emotions held down all this time could be expressed and I could heal.

I realized that I also had a belief that love could break my heart. Now I have come into an understanding that love cracks the hardness of the heart to let life in. This process of living can also bring pain. But living without love is certainly more painful. A heart can feel like it is broken, but actually it is becoming freer. I had decided not to love again because it was too painful. That took longer to heal. I first had to learn to love myself to let love in. I remember hearing Brad Brown say something about love in a Life Training event. It makes perfect sense now, although it didn't then. 'The absence of love means something else is present, and most of the time it is not nice.' What I understand now is love is like heaven and the something else is hell.

I feel I am trusting love. I have come into an understanding of trust and how that feels like 'heaven' to me. To trust love is not being naïve. When I am naïve I ignore my intuition and all the information that has come my way. By trusting I am able to take in all of the situation no matter how negative it may seem and begin to turn the situation around to make it an advantage. It's the old 'If life gives you lemons, then make lemonade' philosophy. When I trust I am using the power of my mind to be objective so that I can see and experience the positive that is in all situations. By trusting it gives me clarity. I am responding into life. Not trusting is reaction. I think people often confuse love with need. When our needs are not met, it hurts. Love never hurts.

Reiki has been one of the biggest instruments I have used in my return to love. To me, Reiki energy is unconditional love. Love is in the centre of all things. Love is the light of God. When we react we move away from the light and from love. When we respond we come back home. Giving myself Reiki energy is like opening the door to my heart and to heaven. The experience of this is one I have come to trust with certainty.

Do you trust love? What personal pain have you moved through to have life and love reside in you again?

_____

_____

_____

_____

If you do not trust love, what can you start to do so that you will?

_____

_____

_____

_____

Have you forgiven yourself?

_____

_____

_____

_____

Waiting for Mr Right

Years ago, I remember saying to a friend of mine that I was afraid to love again. My marriage took a lot out of me when it broke up. My trust had been shattered. I doubted myself as a sexual being and felt that only if the right man came along would I be so exposed with my feelings again. I was justified to wait until Mr Right arrived to take me away from my pain and give me reason to live. Years passed and I was beginning to doubt that Mr Right would come. I thought perhaps he had lost his way or that the map to reach me was unclear. I was sitting and meditating one morning and had a question, just who is Mr Right? From the deepest part of my being I heard, 'All are Mr Right, there is simply no Mr Wrong.' How much I had missed by not allowing myself to see the perfection and rightness in all men that had come into my life. By not allowing myself to be in a loving relationship with men I had also not allowed men to be in a loving relationship with me. Now when I am seeing the vast beauty and uniqueness of people I hear myself say, 'All are right, there are no wrongs!'

Have you been waiting for the perfect person or circumstance to enter your life before you do something? Have you put your life on hold waiting to win the lottery or achieve that result? What do you suppose you are missing that can fulfil you?

_____

_____

_____

_____

What must you decide to do in order for another person to take their loving place beside you?

_____

_____

_____

_____

Awakening to Love

On the rarest occasions, a person can happen into our lives at such a time to awaken us to our positive loving side. When this has happened we then feel close enough to not only share all the things that have brought us pain and thus helped us to grow, but also what now brings us laughter, fun and deep enjoyment by being together. The positive and loving aspects of ourselves that have been tucked away and not enjoyed or allowed to be explored for some time become the parts of our core personality that we develop more because of being with one another. If the person then goes away from our life we draw on these shared memories to keep this part of ourselves present. We continue to explore and enjoy the newness we have experienced in others and ourselves as a result of our coming together. To have this happen even for a short while gives rise in us the possibility for it to continue and deepen not only in ourselves but also in the person who has touched our life in such a way. We have been blessed and are a blessing.

Have you opened friendship's door to awaken yourself to love?

_____

_____

_____

_____

What new and positive belief structures have you put into place to support you to keep your heart open?

_____

_____

_____

_____

I felt like I had been in this doorway to love for quite a while. I had seen and felt my early decisions about love and how my not loving had cut me off from living. I wondered where were the new thoughts I had been putting into place. Certainly there was a book somewhere that contained my new wisdom and understanding.

My darling child, is it so necessary to have a book to hold in your hand to make sure you remember what is true for you now concerning love? For how big is a book? How many pages would you need to write all you now know? And then would you need to carry it around with you so you would not forget? Would it get heavy after a while and left beside the road to make your journey lighter? What are these new realizations?

Where can you keep them so you will remember?

I have some new thoughts pertaining to love and how to achieve it, grandmother. These new thoughts have been coming with each memory I have reviewed here in this time. I see that changing my mind from my conditioned reaction that was formed in the past will allow me to experience life differently. It will give me a place to build from that has truths that support me in my grace and majesty.

I see that my mind has been afraid of change. It does not like the unknown and would do anything to hold on to what it knows, even if what it is holding on to is hell. I understand that by being willing to change the first step has already been taken. Even without necessarily knowing the outcome I have trusted enough to make a move. This step has also required my faith. Trust and faith have melted the fear that kept me frozen in the past.

Also that by feeling my feelings it gives me permission to be associated with life and to participate in a more loving and natural way. My natural tendency was to shut down and be in control. This rooted me firmly in an independent role. Of course my fear was exactly opposite, that I would be dependent and no one would be there for me, or would leave me when they could. I moved to the other side of polarity in order not to be dependent. I also touched into how I used emotions and the demonstration of them to get what I wanted. This was quite hard for me to see about myself and yet at the same time very freeing. When I was dependent I was little and needed to be rescued. My language and emotions were of a pitiful nature. I loathed this about myself so decided I would not express my feelings, I would be strong and never need anyone. This took much of my personal energy to keep in place because inside was the frightened little girl who did need and I could not respond to her. So the surface of me was not truthful. It was a mask I wore to protect me, even from myself.

I have learned that the truest form of self-love is to come into the centre, which is interdependence. I am then reassociated with my feelings. If I have what I would hold as a negative emotion I can then release it and let more positive feeling in. I am in the centre where love is.

I have experienced that commitment to myself is taking the time necessary to prioritize what I do to include myself in my life. That this is an act of love. Being driven to do is actually a means to keep myself separate from love. Commitment is not from sacrifice, rather from response. When I am in a committed relationship with myself I am putting my needs first. When I am in a committed relationship with another, I am naturally putting this person's needs first to bring them joy. In this experience I am also filled with joy. Commitment is not to be feared, rather to be embraced. The tool I need to keep myself free, that will therefore also shift any problem I may have, is trust and forgiveness. They are essentially the keys to open the door to love. Once the door has been opened it will move me forward into intimacy.

When I am in this 'in-to-me-see' energy my barriers will have melted and I abide in the compassionate heart. This intimacy that love has made manifest has the power to heal all my problems. My problems involve thoughts that separate me from wholeness. A problem is also a reaction and most of the time has to do with need rather than love. The power of intimacy and love transforms the need to be separate. Intimacy therefore should not be confused with romance, which is often based on unrealistic dreams. It is a sharing of the heart and mind in such a way that it literally empowers each other to be real and more intimate. In this space there is a joining and a new reference to live life from. I have said Yes to life and loving. I in that moment live in heaven right here on earth.

Well done my child! So if you were to write all that in a book what would the title be? But, most of all my child, how would all these realizations feel in your body?

Grandmother, I do love you. I wouldn't need a book or a title. The feelings associated with living my new truths would be the touchstone to always remember. I would feel free and happy from the centre of my being, deep in my heart.

Essentially, how do you see yourself in relationship to trust, forgiveness and intimacy?

_____

_____

_____

_____

How had you decided you needed to be to feel safe?

_____

_____

_____

_____

Knowing what you do about yourself now, do you still need these things? Have you decided to change your mind?

_____

_____

_____

_____

What priorities will you set for yourself?

_____

_____

_____

_____

Can you be in a committed relationship? What have you done to be ready for this step in your life?

_____

_____

_____

_____

Finally, I have a beautiful message that sits on my desk written by a spiritual teacher from India. His name was Meher Baba, which translates as Compassionate Father. A man who stayed beside him for many years and is now in the world reminding people of their greatness gave this to me. His name is Moonie Baba, which translates into Silent Father. Both men had taken a vow of silence. Both men with their writing and deeds have invited us to live in the centre where love is.

Love has to spring spontaneously from within; it is in no way amenable to any form of inner or outer force. Love and coercion can never go together; but while love cannot be forced upon anyone, it can awaken through love itself. Love is essentially self-communicative; those who receive love from others cannot be its recipients without giving a response that, in itself, is the nature of love. True love is unconquerable and irresistible. It goes on gathering power and spreading itself until it eventually transforms everyone it touches. Humanity will attain a new mode of being and life through the free and unhampered interplay of pure love from heart to heart.

Meher Baba

After answering the questions, take time to sit quietly and feel your body. Remember that revisiting areas of your life may also bring up emotions that you may not have expressed in a long time. Take the time to give yourself a self-treatment. By loving into yourself you set these emotions free and acknowledge the importance of each step you have taken.

Close your eyes and take a deep, cleansing breath. Feel your body. Are there areas that are tight or heavy? Are there places in you that need to be touched and loved into? Use your hands to touch these places. Give yourself Reiki to return these areas into harmony. If you have been initiated into Reiki two energy, use the power and emotional mental symbols to work deeply to return yourself to a state of inner harmony and peace.

Honour yourself and your journey thus far.

THE DOORWAY
OF MATURITY

I HAVE wrestled with this word maturity for days. I know that to come into inner peace my attitude towards maturity needs to be in harmony. But, is it only just about getting older? Is there something more about being mature, and what does this look and feel like?

I felt old all my life. Not old in my body, but old in my mind. When I was younger I found that I did not have much in common with people my own age. I felt so much better with people 10 to 20 years older, even though I thought my parents, at 40, were old. It was a matter of my perspective, and my friends were not my parents.

I had been expected to be mature growing up. I was responsible for my decisions and myself. I was taught to think of others and to have a strong work ethic. I imagine it was part of being in the particular family I was raised in, being the oldest child and therefore expected to set an example, caring for my mom and, of course, my early decisions as to how I had to be to survive in the world.

I started getting tired. The more I thought about maturity, the more my mind wanted to stop and just sleep. What was I trying to avoid in this doorway?

You see, my child, when you search your mind for information, the mind says that you are up to something no good. Based on the previous experiences it has had of you writing this book it says you will be making changes. It is afraid because one more stronghold may crumble and then what? So the mind's fear of the unknown will induce you to sleep and tell you that you can think of this tomorrow, better yet next year, or if you don't think about it then it may go away. Will you continue to curl up on your bed or wake up and notice your mind is winning over your heart? When you have noticed that is happening then what will you do? What is your intention for writing this book?

Please grandmother, I am entitled to have a nap just like everyone. I just need some time to sort my thoughts out. My eyes are feeling so heavy. Give me a break.

Who needs to give whom a break, dear one? I am asking you in this moment, are you supporting yourself into your majesty and grace or into your darkness? If you are supporting yourself to be asleep, or dark, perhaps it is you who needs to give yourself a break from this conditioned behaviour.

I have a question for you. Who is the oneness and is it other than you? You do things that bring you separation from this out of your fear.

OK, I will answer your question. I am writing this book to help people by sharing my personal journey so that they, the reader, may also see which doorways they have closed with their reactions that also have blocked the energy for the Spirit to work though them. Conceivably, this book will serve as a key to unlock the doors and bring them into closer relationship with their divine nature, the light and the oneness. I understand that I am probably tired because I am being resistant to looking here to see what may be true. Or I could see that what I have said before is no longer valid and decide that it is time to have some new beliefs that support me in my being light. I am realizing, too, that the process of writing the book is also bringing up more for me to clear and choose from. My own process is going deeper. Throughout this experience of writing I also am determining the stepping stones I may be on in regards to the individual doorways. I am drawn into the realization that everything I do involves the whole, which includes me, one more time. Everything thus supports me into my light; it is my fear that supports me into my darkness.

Yes, that is a probability. So what is it about maturity that you do not want to see?

My first thoughts are that if I am mature then I am old. Because of this thinking I am put into direct relationship with my mortality. Maturity also means I have to be responsible, I stop having fun because I have to be grown up. My goodness, I wonder where that all came from? As a child I had to act older. I did have more responsibility and not as much fun as I would have liked. But, now I also see that I may not have been acting maturely. Maturity is not about how old I am. It is about the decisions I make. I think being mature is being in the centre of my being, using all information and intuition available and deciding things for myself with an understanding of how this affects all others. It is having guardianship.

Where is this new thinking or feeling coming from? On one side, you can see and feel that being mature is not fun and then, on the other side, you also see great possibilities. How can this be so?

I believe that when I am reactionary there are certain feelings in my body that I can identify depending on the emotion and thoughts I am experiencing. I was feeling fatigued, sleepy and cross. I can choose to breathe and come above the situation to get a different perspective on a situation, in this case why I was resistant to writing about maturity. You were reminding me of my overall purpose for doing this book. You continued to evoke me to be awake by asking me what behaviour I was supporting. That got my attention. So at that point I chose to be more objective. I could listen to my mind telling me those things but also see other possibilities. This is maturity; having the ability to discern and understanding that my choices ultimately affect the whole. What is interesting is when I could see both I had no attachment to either, and yet when I made the choice for the new truth my body was flooded with a sense of peace and light. I had moved into the centre of my being.

Which feels better? And which one do you have more experiences of?

Obviously, it feels better to move into the centre of my being, as I am more alive then. I have had many experiences being in the other state or death. It does not energize my body, mind or spirit being there. The whole journey for me is one of giving myself experiences that continue to build on the feelings of being light, centred and alive. The more experience I have of being enlightened, then when I am not light, the quicker I will feel when to make a choice to change. This is being awake. I am giving myself more and more light-building experiences. Reiki has been so instrumental in this. When I feel dark or reactionary I can respond with my hands to touch those places on my body and give energy to them. The result is relaxation and peace.

Given you have had thoughts about maturity not being a state you would like to reach too soon, would you please tell me when your mind made those beliefs and what are the experiences that you have had to make your new belief structures?

I had prayed for guidance to come to terms with maturity. To re-experience and be shown decision-making moments so that I could clear these thoughts. What held those beliefs in place that did not support me and what experiences created my new belief structure?

I was falling back in time and space. I saw before me a time in my life in which I had decided that life is not fun when you are older.

Dinner time

At times my parents' relationship could be violent. Dinner time was when feelings and tempers could escalate very easily. I remember moments when my brother Scott and I witnessed something that resembled a tennis match played by our parents consisting of words volleyed back and forth to each other. Other times, we experienced the icy silence of resentment.

One evening at dinner, things elevated past icy and erupted into fully-fledged anger. I do not remember the words that they were using. What I remember is that a full plate of spaghetti and sauce went flying across the table and landed directly in my father's face. My brother and I ran from the room as we both felt that total war had been declared in that moment and we both wanted to be out of the line of fire.

Later on we heard the front door slam. We came out of our rooms to find our dad shaken and mother gone. I was worried that mom would do something to hurt herself and so I sat up all night waiting for her to come home. Eventually, dad and my brother went to bed. The house was quiet, yet inside I was in turmoil. I needed someone to give me guidance about how to help my parents. And more importantly, some insight about how not to be the same way when I got older. I felt I must be the mature one of our family, yet did not have even the common sense I needed for myself.

My mother did not return that night. I went out in the early morning to try and find her. She was asleep under the bushes in front of the house. I was relieved to find her and embarrassed that all the neighbours would have seen her there. I did not realize then what a statement she was making by doing that. She had wanted to be seen and pitied. Her role as a martyr propelled her into this type of reaction. I woke her up and brought her into the house and into my bed. I remember holding her close and letting her cry. I was 13 years old at the time. I decided then that being old enough to have kids was not fun at all.

What are your thoughts about maturity now?

At what age should one be mature and why do you think so?

What memories do you have of times your parents or family members did not act maturely, and what early decisions did you make regarding maturity?

_____

_____

_____

_____

Coming of Age

My daughter Stacey was almost 18 when she made the decision to leave home and start her 'adult' life with a girlfriend in their own apartment. She found a job after she completed high school. She did not want to go to college. She was anxious to get on with her life. After her stepfather Ken left and we had a few years of battle, things had been settling down. I was going through my own process of my baby leaving home and the dreaded empty nest syndrome. Stacey took me to the apartment complex where she and Velma were going to rent their apartment. We looked at the model apartment so I had an idea of what theirs would look like when one became available. I decided to help her as much as I could and began buying dishes and things for the house. It was fun talking to her about what she wanted. She had very strong ideas about colour and style at her age.

I had myself emotionally ready for the day she would be leaving. I had planned a nice dinner the night before she would go and some time for completion. Everything was set in my head. I went away for a Life Training weekend on a Friday night three weeks before she was to move and told her I would be back on Sunday late. I remember telling her, 'I love you and have a great weekend.' When I returned late on Sunday night she had moved out. Her room was empty, closets stripped bare, her bathroom devoid of her things, and all the stuff I had purchased for her new home had also been taken away. The house, normally alive and warm, was cold and empty. I could not believe that she had not told me she was leaving then. There was a note on the bar in the kitchen. It read, 'Mom, I am sorry, I just had to go. I know you will be upset, it is just something I've got to do now. I will call you when I am settled in. Love Stacey.' In one moment I went from happy to be home to my God what did I do for her to leave like this? I took it as my fault she had gone the same as I had blamed myself when Ken left. I felt my life had been turned upside down.

I survived the night with the help of a friend. Days moved forward as I adjusted to living alone again. It seemed like the house and I became friends. I closed off the part that was empty. I started doing things to make me feel more content. Flowers in vases, music I liked to hear, all became my therapy to return to my centre.

Stacey called at the office and asked me to dinner at her house. I gratefully accepted and went there at the appointed time. Their home was beautiful and reflected them both. I was struck that Stacey's bedroom that had normally been messy was in this house spotlessly clean. She fixed a nice meal and we had a good conversation. She filled me in on her life since she had gone. She explained to me that she felt I would be too emotional when she left for her to handle, so that by leaving this way it would be better for us both. She had forgotten that when I was in control no emotions would show. At the end of the evening she said, 'You know Mom, growing up isn't all it is cracked up to be. Being an adult means I must work my job, clean house, cook meals, do my laundry, worry about money, and there is no one to hold me to say it will be all right. I had no idea it would be so hard. I don't know how you have managed, especially with daddy Ken gone. It is a lot of responsibility.'

I smiled at my daughter and knew she was acknowledging me in her way for taking care of her, especially after Ken left. It was not always easy. I said, 'You know honey, becoming an adult is like taking a cruise. We get all excited about planning the trip; we purchase the ticket and show up to get onboard. Everyone sees us off. The gangplank is taken away and we sail off into the sunset. The only problem is that they have not told us the ship never docks again. We are on this boat for the rest of our lives. There is everything we need to be an adult, or to grow into one if we got on too early. If we decide this cruise isn't much fun, then the journey will be reflected that way. It is just how you want to see it. It is really up to you if you enjoy your life, but there is no going back.' My daughter gave me a big hug and said, 'I have missed your wisdom, mom. I love you.'

Sometimes decisions that may seem immature, such as leaving before a committed time, can lead to wisdom and maturity. My daughter had taken a leap out of the nest. We both had time to heal and could acknowledge the changes and gifts in each other.

It was a very empowering evening for both of us. I accepted and encouraged my daughter in her choice. She knew I was there if she needed me. I knew where she was and that she had begun her new journey as a woman separate from me. As for myself, my maturity came when I could see this and accept it as so. I had no hold on anything. I wished both of us well.

If you are a parent, has your child or children left home? If so, describe the feelings you went through.

_____

_____

_____

_____

When you left home, what were your feelings and the circumstances around your departure? Did you ever go back home?

_____

_____

_____

_____

Let us imagine you were going to leave home again. Would you do it differently than last time and why?

_____

_____

_____

_____

The Tree Does not Worry

We all had gathered for the professional level seminar in a beautiful castle in Liblice, in the northern region of the Czech Republic called Bohemia. We came from all areas of this beautiful country including one student who came from the Netherlands to join us. We were full of anticipation and wonder. Most of us had not seen each other for a year. We had previously been together in the Nine-month Programme the year before and had grown so much together and personally. We came with questions. We wanted some insight during these 12 days together. Some questions were: should I leave my present job? What will I do now that I am no longer in a relationship? What is stopping me from having what I want? and so on. The first day was filled with telling our story, sharing things we would not normally do. We felt safe in this environment of love and compassion. Our hearts broke open, tears were spent, laughter shared and a bonding occurred in the room during the first hours of the course. When we went inside during a meditation for the answers to our questions, most of us found the reason why we were questioning in the first place was because we had fear. So, quite naturally, our next question was why do we fear so much, especially since we know it cuts us off from our creative essence? Many of us had touched into a fear of not having enough abundance in our lives. The country was in recession and so many changes were happening quickly. Most of us didn't feel we were standing on stable ground.

My friend Nick Price had come from Scotland to co-teach with me for the first few days of the course. He had said his fear was not having enough money and that it was a major problem in his life. He said, 'I know there is abundance all around me. I look out to the trees and they are full of leaves. The leaves are green and represent money or currency. Currency is like a circuit flowing freely to and fro like electricity. I am the one who stops the flow with my fear. Why?'

I sat there for a moment and saw so clearly a picture in my mind. I said to the group and Nick, 'The tree does not care if it has leaves or not. It does not care if birds come to roost in its branches or how many come if they do. It has no worry about the weather. It is simply and profoundly being all it came here to be, which is a tree. The tree accepts everything that happens. Everything is part of its experience being a tree. Basically, the tree does not worry.' The course took on a theme from that day. When we would get stuck and wonder why, someone would say lovingly, 'The tree does not worry.' It was a sign to let go of the past and be present in the moment. There is maturity in being present that does not necessarily come with age. We learn to be all that we came to be just as the tree.

What have been your recent worries or fears?

_____

_____

_____

_____

Let's suppose you have the answer to why you are troubled. What is that answer?

_____

_____

_____

_____

How much of you is present when you are afraid?

_____

_____

_____

_____

Out of the centre of yourself where your maturity is available to you, what advice would you give yourself?

_____

_____

_____

_____

I sat and stretched, returning to a more conscious state. I had been shown some events in my life in which the previously held beliefs I had about maturity were no longer valid. I wondered where my new beliefs would lead me. How could I integrate this newness into my life? I felt full of warmth and had a strong desire to give out of a new part of myself, but what?

My child, what is it you want to give from the centre of yourself? Let go and create what that would be. Allow yourself to feel and to taste it as if this were here and now.

I see before us a world of beauty beyond our wildest dreams. Each and every person is honoured and respected for who they are and the gifts that they bring to the whole. We see that light reflects light just as the darkness reflects darkness. That all is a matter of choice. We can create our hell or heaven right here on the earth. We support and empower each other into our majesty. We walk beside our brothers and sisters. We understand that we are all interconnected and that what we do affects the whole. We take the time to be in relationship with nature. We learn from the animals, flowers and even the wind. We do not measure a man or woman's worth by the size of his or her house. Rather, it is the qualities of the heart that are held as pure gold and are indeed a precious treasure.

What do I want to give from the centre of myself, you ask. Simply myself as authentic as I can be in each moment. To demonstrate wisdom by living my life as full of joy and love as I will allow in each moment. When I react to clear my mind and to move back into the centre where love is and fear has no place. To remember to be like the tree, not concerned with how many leaves I have or birds that roost in my branches, rather to be all I came to be which is a magnificent human being.

And what will you need to remember all that you have seen and said here, my child?

I need to keep as a source how being in the centre of my being feels so that when I am not in my centre I will have a point of reference to move back to. Also, I believe that honouring myself for wherever I am in the moment is important, as it is all part of my process. Accept others and myself as they are. Hold the space for them to make their own movement and in their own time. Weed my own garden first basically, and not be concerned about the garden of my neighbour. However, I know also in maturity there is a deep consciousness that we are all part of the whole and the guardianship is to be aware of our actions and reactions and how they affect the whole. I believe that with maturity comes the wisdom to be more and do less.

From the centre of your being, what is it that you want for yourself and our world?

_____
_____
_____
_____

And how will you remember what you have said and felt here?

_____
_____
_____
_____

In December 1989 I had been given a message from grandmother. She said:

My child, often you have come to the well wondering if it is safe to drink the water of life. You have waited for someone to draw up the water so that you may drink. I invite you to draw your own water, be your own source of divine inspiration. You can put your hand in the water and drink as often as you like. Act as your heart implies, not as your mind disposes you to. Nothing has to make sense in the realm of the mind. It must feel true to you in your heart. Open up to all life's majesty and experiences. It is time to put your very good reasons aside and step into the light of which you are. Walk in this light and feel the beloved. The God in you welcomes the mother and the father. The God in you sees all else as God and one. You have asked what are you afraid of. You are afraid of your brilliance. Yet when you do not shine brightly you also do not give the space for others to be bright. Majesty evokes majesty. Know, my darling child, that the pathway before you is like the golden steps to father's side. Remember when you said I trust you mother/father/God? You took steps to them. Did you think that the steps could only be walked on in one direction? For they come to you too. Come to that place inside you and be nourished as you continue to nourish others. Drink from a full cup and sit beside us and feel the support and love of all those who walk beside you in love.

Sometimes we need to hear the message life brings us many times to finally 'get it'. I am grateful that I heard this and now, with maturity, I have chosen to respond with love.

霊

気

THE DOORWAY
HOME

I REMEMBER seeing a needlework sampler hanging in my grandmother's kitchen with the words, 'Home is where the heart is'. When I was younger I thought, wherever we were, home was there because we took our hearts with us when we travelled. This is true, for in every moment we can and do create a home for ourselves. We have an internal and an external home. Some homes are more comfortable than others. We create our physical home responding to what we feel our needs to be comfortable are. We may also go through phases in our lives in which we find we need very little, and possibly later we will swing over to the other polarity of needing quite a lot to feel comfortable or complete. Some have come into a middle point. What was important to me when I rented my flat in the Czech Republic was that I bought a bed that was comfortable. Every time I come back from travelling, I lay on my bed and exclaimed, 'I am home, yea!'

Some of us go through phases of needing to make a statement about our worth and tie our self-esteem up in our material possessions. We get busy acquiring things like a car, bigger house, nice sound system, jewellery and so on. When I went through this many years ago, I started thinking that I needed a bigger house to hold all my things, and then realized it would just fill up again. I took the time to go inside and see what need was not being met that I thought I was filling up with goods. When I realized what it was I could let go of things, have less and be happier.

Our societies in the West play on our insecurity. I have spent a lot of time listening to what people feel they need to be happy. The answers are varied yet follow a theme of having a better job, a relationship and being financially secure. Most of the time it is not the quality of living that they address, it is the things they think they must have so others will think they are something more. A man who wants a relationship may think he needs the relationship to be with a glamorous big-breasted woman, possibly so that other men will envy him. He also feels younger and virile when he has this 'babe' on his arm. The picture he has created in his mind says he is 'something better' to have a good-looking woman like that. So we attempt to complete ourselves or make ourselves look better through things or other people. We then have lost the opportunity to have deep and meaningful relationships because we are not fully available to engage in one. We are only available to be completed or complemented. When we have unresolved issues with, say, our mother and perhaps have a bad general picture of women, we will use them to satisfy our needs and then discard them. I have found that the overall fear in most of our society is that of being intimate. To establish and maintain a space of seeing deeply into another also requires that you allow yourself to be seen and experienced including the self behind the masks. Can you or would you even want to be intimate with a showpiece that serves to get you noticed? If you are looking only for feeling better about yourself, I would imagine true intimacy would be hard to come by because you would not want to be intimate even with yourself, much less with another person. If you cannot love yourself, how can you allow others to be intimate with you? It would be too threatening. When we start to judge all society on the type of car they drive, their work and bank account balance, we truly miss the experience of the person through the compassionate heart. When we allow compassion we can also have intimacy.

I had a telephone conversation lately with a man who has been a lovely support for me. He is going through a rather difficult phase in his life and is having trouble seeing what also is beautiful and filled with hope in his life. He sees all women as packaged opportunists who are only looking for money and the men who can give them what they want. He is so self-righteously sure that all women are this way that he cannot see that with this mind-set he continues to create these very women to be in his life. And because he does not see his value and gifts, only what he does not have to make him this man to be admired, he continues to bring these opportunities to choose to reinforce his low self-esteem. This is a home that he has made for himself that I pray will get uncomfortable for him soon so he feels he has to make changes. I personally had a hard time listening to his truth about women. I am a woman and felt I had been put into the same category. It became physically painful to hear him. I had to disengage from the conversation. It was so against what I teach and live by. I see him. I love and acknowledge the man in him. He is entitled to his belief structure. My choice becomes to be around him or not. I am now taking the time to see where I may be so fixed about a belief. Do I do the same thing in regards to men or something else? I do not see it now. I will keep looking and using the reflection of the mirror of my friend to light my personal work.

Often times we are so stuck in our stuff we do not even see how others react to it. When we wake up to how we hold others and ourselves as less than light and feel the pain of this separation, we can choose to create new realities. We can create a new place or home to hold our heart and love. Our minds have no grey space and certainly no room for compromise. It is either good or bad. For instance, when we judge women as being a certain way, the mind says all women are like this. When we have not handled our issues around something, be it women or men and ourselves, we normally return to times when we have been stuck about these issues in our various stages of development. Supposing we return to an adolescent time concerning our problem. Normally teenagers need to be in a group to feel stronger and more justified so we will also search for others that have the same belief about our theme. It is more comfortable to be together with the same belief structure. There is a power in unity. We get into co-operative agreement about our thoughts. If enough of us believe this way, we as a community, as a nation, as a world, will create this very thing we give our minds energy for. It isn't about women or men, it is about the collective consciousness of the whole, or the collective unconsciousness.

We can create out of fear or out of love, darkness or light. Both are available to us and we choose in every moment what to create. What is it we are wanting in our lives, in the lives of our families, communities, nations and the world? Will we create fear-based societies that must defend or ones that work for the common good of all concerned? We are being called out in every moment to embrace the big picture, unity and oneness. It takes commitment and certainly love to create peace. It starts in the individual and radiates outwards first. By starting with ourselves we clean and tidy our personal home inside. Of course, what is interesting is that often our actual home environment will reflect our inner process. When we work to come home into ourselves, it also allows space for others to come home into themselves, as there is a release of tension.

Homecoming

I closed my eyes and sat back. My thoughts were racing ahead of me. I could feel my body full of passion about wanting to go home again, the feelings associated with coming home, and a homecoming.

My eyes focused on a homecoming scene I have experienced many times throughout my life. I walked up the golden steps leading from the entrance hall to the main floor. The rooms were filled with light. The smell of white flowers permeated the air, and in the courtyard the songs of birds were so beautiful. It was so good to be home again. My heart was full of love and happiness. Home, I always looked forward to these times to be together again. I was filled with anticipation and a longing to be enfolded in their arms and held. I never tired of being loved and upheld when I was here. I had been gone a long while and I had so much to share with my mother and father. As I reached the top step mother came and took me in her arms, and as she held me close she said, 'Welcome home my daughter. You have been away for so long, I am sure you have much to tell us and I am wanting to hold you close and feel you next to me.' Then father came into the room and took me in his arms welcoming me. I felt his gentle strength and love. I was home in the deepest sense of the word. After a while it was time for me to leave home and start a new journey. Mother and father asked me if I had all I needed. I looked at my hands and said, 'I have all that I need,' as I walked down the stairs back into my life as it was at that time.

When I was a little girl and I would experience this homecoming, I knew that I had gone home to God. God to me has always been God the mother and God the father.

It usually occurred when I was sleeping in the early morning hours. I would always awake refreshed and full of hope. I had been held, loved and reminded of my purpose.

When I was older and explained this to my therapist, I was told I had created the perfect mother and father to replace the earthly ones I had that could not love me as I desired. He basically said it was a fantasy. On the surface I acted like I had given in and let him believe that I understood. I knew that he did not comprehend that I had been going home like this all my life. It isn't easy to talk about something so personal and so spiritual. It was my relationship with God and so precious. No one needed to realize. I knew and that was enough.

Now that I have gotten older I have started sharing these experiences so that people can see that, whatever their relationship is with God or a higher power, it is fine. It is my intention to share this relationship in such a natural and grounded way so that it can be touched. I bring my experience home to them.

You Must Go Home

When I was 21 I had my first near-death experience. I had to have emergency surgery, and in the recovery room I heard them say that they lost me. Well, actually, I was not lost. I had gone home again. I remember looking down at my body lying on the bed; the doctors and nurses were working on me. I floated around the room looking at all the other people there. I went out of the room through the wall at the opposite corner near the top of the ceiling. I knew I was on my way to the golden stairs and home. I went through a beautiful tunnel of light. I had no pain, only a deep sense of love and wholeness. I saw the doors before me; I knew that soon I would be in the reception area and in their arms. Then there was a hand that stopped me. It did not touch me or hold me back; it refused me entrance to go through the door. I fell backwards through the tunnel and came back into my body. The pain was agonizing. I heard, 'We have her back, doctor.' When I could talk and was stable, they asked me if I wanted to see my husband. I only wanted to pray. I knew that there was some reason I had been sent back. I had to inhabit my earthly home longer. It took three months in the hospital to recover physically from the surgery. The doctors called my family and said they did not think I would make it out of the hospital. I was still near death. All during that time I was constantly aware of angels and smelled white flowers. Although I was here, I was being reminded that I was taken care of and loved. I lived in a rural town in Georgia right smack in the middle of the Bible Belt of the South. I could not talk about my experiences. They would think I was crazy. But they did understand prayer, and all their prayers sustained me as I moved back into health and living in my body again. I never feared death after that experience. It is a homecoming without pain and contains absolute knowing. I also knew that there was something to do here on Earth. My God, the mother and father, wanted me here, and I could still go back for visits but not to live yet.

A look at the Future through the Eyes of my Child

When Stacey was very little I explained to her that God had sent me back to Earth so that I could take care of her. She had heard from the family that I had been dead for five minutes and that it was a miracle I was still alive. She was naturally inquisitive and seemed satisfied that I had come back to take care of her. One day, she was playing and looked up at me and said, 'Mom, you came back for more than just me.'

We went to see a movie many years later. It was *Resurrection*. The story was about a woman who had been in an automobile accident and had a death experience. She came back into her body with the power to heal given to her as a gift. The movie centred on how she came to terms with the gift. It is a beautiful and evoking movie. Stacey took hold of my hand while we were watching the movie and said, 'Mommie, I know why you came back now. You came to heal people just like her, only you will help to heal their hearts too.'

I had no idea how intuitive she was at the time, for indeed I use my hands for others to heal themselves, and the work I lead in the extended programmes very much centres on the heart and coming home to ourselves with love. I never was told this is what I had come back to do by God. I seemed to gravitate towards this work like a moth goes towards the flame. God is my greatest cheerleader, watching how I continue to choose the steps I will take. I always have free will choice. I created the opportunities that gave me the choices I have made. I am grateful to be in the practice of Reiki.

I decided I wanted to stretch my body and have a walk in nature. I was looking for more wisdom about home and coming home. I walked down the walkway to the small lake at the back of the castle where I was teaching and writing. There was a beautiful grove of old tress. I spread my blanket at the base of a tree and sat down with my back resting against the trunk. I felt my body relax. I began to hear even the grass grow, so silent I had become and in tune with nature.

I welcome you home, my child. Although you do not often think of here as your home in a spiritual sense, it is, and such a glorious home at that. For when you truly surrender into the oneness you will experience a home-coming on all levels. There will be no doubt that you are home, wherever you may think or experience yourself being. Do you remember your near-death experiences? You had a profound sense of knowing. What did you know and how long did it last?

I knew all, not with my mind but with my being. There were no questions. I was everything so I knew totally out of my experience of being all there is. This is also the same experience I had in Poland when I had the initiation and subsequent 21 days of bliss. But they all went away eventually. I can access it again. However, it is not with the same intensity or absolute surrender. I have thought about this often as I love being there, but it seemed to me that it was too much to sustain. I needed to experience non-bliss to enjoy the bliss, if that makes sense to you. In a more earthy sense, if all I did were have orgasm after orgasm with no break in between, I would cease to know when I was having one. The cycle needs space of no orgasm to experience the completion of orgasm. There is an ebb and flow. But I also wonder if we do reach a state of bliss that can be sustained.

The bliss, dear one, is in knowing that it is there. When you cease to struggle to get it, then it will come to you. The surrender is when you stop seeing and experiencing yourself separate from all that is. In order to experience all you must also have an experience of the opposite, or nothing. It is not becoming frustrated when you do not sustain the feeling; it is having joy that you can experience it again and again. Remember when you said our spiritual work is like lighting a light in our souls to come back to? This is the same thing. We always can come home. Home is on many levels.

If you wish for understanding and love in your life, then give these away without demand. The act of giving creates what it is you are wanting. So in order to experience the bliss, you must give bliss out of your being. What would giving bliss to others look like to you?

I imagine it would look like giving acknowledgement about their gifts, loving them honestly, giving them the space to be who they are without asking them to change, empowering them into their light and reminding them who they are. I would imagine that creating bliss for myself is in the act of giving people back to themselves.

Exactly! So do you see that you are in bliss even when you do not realize it? When you are doing and being 'the work', as you call it, is this not bliss? For what do you experience when you see that they have come home to themselves? What is the nectar that comes forth when others are alive in their light?

I experience myself as light and I have moved from the perspective of home for one, myself, which is an internal home, to that of a communal one. The home becomes bigger. Now I also see that when we as a group or nation of people are creating this bliss for others, we uphold more people to find themselves and our home becomes even larger. In fact, it is unlimited, or as limited as our minds will create it to be. But why is it that we forget we can do this?

Dear one, with every forgetting there is a remembering. Each and every time you are caused to remember and have others awaken to their selves, the light of love will grow stronger. As you take up the call to give bliss to others, you continue to remember that your truest purpose, in fact, the truest purpose of all, is to help heal the hurts of those wounded. Give relief to those who fear, and dance in the light of all that you are, which is God. Keep giving yourself the experience of your light and the light will grow stronger. When you get upset that you have forgotten, then you become darker. Again it is your choice always.

Many times I have sat with you, people have come to hear my wisdom, yet this is ageless, timeless wisdom that is not mine. It is the same message said by many aspects of God. We keep repeating the message in hopes that you will remember. When I say you are the light, hold your flame high to show them the way home. Do you suppose I am saying there are one or two that walk beside you? No, my darlings, there are many illuminated by the light of God indwelling in you. Your radiance is so divinely brilliant. Because of you, many are warmed and awakened in their hearts to remember and come home. You who are reading this book, I am speaking to you. You are my darlings.

Remember your light and together you will create such a marvellous place to live and such a homecoming will occur. What is it you are wanting? What is home to you? Have you touched into your personal home in your heart and, if so, what was the experience of it? Have you surrendered and become one before? If so, how long did it last? Are you willing to be one who wakes others in the world? What would that look like? Can you even imagine a universal home? Tell me what you imagine?

_____

_____

_____

_____

I awoke as if I had been in a deep slumber. There was a newness that was coursing through me as if I had been charged with a purpose and given a direction to go in. I stood and shook my blanket before folding it up. I started hearing words in my ears. Remember to shine brightly and dance in the light of all that you are...

Help Others to Remember the Way Home

I imagine that God loves us so much that we will keep getting the message over and over again. I have heard grandmother say, 'Help others to remember the way home' for years. Yet it did not seem to touch my soul as deeply as it does now. Perhaps it is because I am remembering more as I write this. All telling of stories gives us a chance to see life differently and awake from a deep sleep. Throughout time, fairy-tales have been used to impart a spiritual message to children. And in the telling of the story the person is also touched. Perhaps it can be as simple as telling the story, our own story, of times we have come home. In the remembering we come home and in the story we help others to remember. I do not think we need to stand on a soapbox and proclaim to the whole community what they need to do. Rather, it is walking in the light that we are. By demonstrating love, compassion and respect we can evoke an awakening without demand. Love touches all and by its very existence transforms. We cannot escape from it for we are it in every moment. I had been touched to remember something that had been buried deep in my mind for all these years. It seemed like a whisper over time and although I heard it so distinctly I did not acknowledge the message until now. I will continue the story.

I had come home from work late, tired, with a mind full of tasks I needed to accomplish before I could go to bed. Stacey had gone to her room to play before dinner; she was always good about sensing I needed space to sort myself out. I started dinner and had the first load of laundry in the washing machine. Her daddy was not home and more than likely would be late. It was summer and everyone had emergency problems with their air conditioning. Since we were in business for ourselves, he always went out when we received a call. I started running the vacuum cleaner over the floor in the living room. I remember thinking, 'I can at least get one room cleaned up.' All of a sudden I felt an overwhelming compulsion to check on Stacey. I turned the vacuum off, walked to her bedroom door, and looked in. She had taken all her dolls and stuffed toys and put them in a semi-circle in front of her. She was sitting in her little red rocker very intently saying, 'It's easy to find your way home when it is dark. You let some of the light in your heart shine out like a flashlight so you don't have to be afraid of the dark.' How did she get to be so wise, this three-and-a-half year-old daughter of mine? Who told her to shine her light? I imagine grandmother had been whispering in her ear or touching her heart. I am so grateful for remembering more of our story. My daughter still helps me to be awake.

What wisdom have your children imparted to you to wake you up?

_____

_____

_____

_____

Please start writing your story to help us all to remember.

_____

_____

_____

_____

After answering the questions, take time to sit quietly and feel your body. Remember that revisiting areas of your life may also bring up emotions that you may not have expressed in a long time. Take the time to give yourself a self-treatment. By loving into yourself you set these emotions free and acknowledge the importance of each step you have taken.

Close your eyes and take a deep, cleansing breath. Feel your body. Are there areas that are tight or heavy? Are there places in you that need to be touched and loved into? Use your hands to touch these places. Give yourself Reiki to return these areas into harmony. If you have been initiated into Reiki two energy, use the power and emotional mental symbols to work deeply to return yourself to a state of inner harmony and peace.

Honour yourself and your journey thus far.

THE DOORWAY OF TRANSFORMATION
AND INNER PEACE

ALL life is a series of change. As we transform our thoughts and feelings, our words and actions take on a different meaning and propel us further along the cycle of life. Change is then like breathing. When we inhale and exhale, life flows and we are constantly in metamorphosis. As we raise our consciousness by transforming old patterns, we also then tap into finer and still finer life force energy and thus our ultimate connection with the source. With a quiet mind that no longer drives us to do, we can sit in the silence and remember to be. This silence is the truest song of the soul; no sweeter music could be experienced. We are sourced and become the sorcerer. We have moved back into our divinity.

Everything we feel, think and act on becomes, as a result, part of the transformational process. We think of transformation as getting closer to our spiritual truth or moving up and away from our shadow. But when we react out of fear and anger we also move closer to our darkness. We thus are constantly experiencing transformation or a change in the quality of our light. The questions are, then, what do we wish to transform to and how do we wish to create ourselves in every moment?

At the beginning of the book I shared some stepping stones that can be experienced in each of the doorways we walk through on the journey home to inner peace. I would like to return to these by looking at them more personally together. By acknowledging some of the times we have stood on the stones, our story can help others to acknowledge the changes they have made in their lives. We could say the experiences of our stones are our Karma yoga. Yoga is a spiritual practice. Living life consciously can be considered a spiritual practice. Karma is the natural and necessary happenings in one's lifetime. In life you always have the choice to make changes. Karma is always present and is the effect of our thinking, emotions and resulting actions. Karma is like the wheel of life that supports us back into the direct relationship with God and the oneness. Let us see where we may be standing or have stood before.

The First Stepping-Stone: Pulling Apart

I have experienced this struggle to keep the status quo many times in my life.

I know that when I was in Scotland working, I started to feel like everything was unravelling at once. The people who owned my flat wanted it back; soon I would have no base in Edinburgh. The work I had been doing with two of the doctors seemed to be drying up. It became harder and harder to live. Yet, I had this demand that everything stay the same. I had to do, have and live in a certain way. Life was pulling apart and I felt I was losing everything I knew and trusted.

When I was married and things were not happy, I still struggled to keep it all together. At the expense of my daughter and myself, I was holding on to an illusion in the hope that something would change. In fact, I was demanding it to be how I saw it had to be. Again, my life was unravelling and I was working hard to tie all the loose ends together.

I realized that the relationship I was working so hard to keep was actually comprised of aspects that did not support either of us. But rather than let it go I demanded somehow it had to all fit and work. It became so painful for both of us to maintain the lie that what we had nourished either one of us. Our relationship was unravelling in front of us.

I had for years refused to feel any emotion. I had made myself so safe and guarded that nothing could get in. When I could no longer control my emotions, my fear was I would go out of control and hurt someone. My life as I had created it could no longer be contained. Something had to change.

What were some of the times you remember when it was just too hard to keep the status quo, when your whole life seemed to want to take a new direction?

_____

_____

_____

_____

The Second Stepping-Stone: Wanting

Having been brought to the point of deciding that I need something different in my life, I have sometimes been at a loss as to what it is I do want. I remember that I was looking for a job. I knew I did not want to do the same thing in exactly the same way, but what did I want to do? I wrote a list of all the things I did not want to do as my life's work. The list was quite long and detailed. Then I took a fresh piece of paper and started writing down the things I did not find on the first list. It was amazing how defined I had made the work I wanted to do. I think that sometimes we are afraid to ask for what we really want. Perhaps our mind says we will not get it anyway, or on the other hand, it may be saying 'If I get what I want, then what will I do?'

When my husband left I decided I wanted my own bed, sheets and blankets. It was important to me that it was just mine and had never contained his energy. I suppose my mind said I didn't want him in bed with me. I noticed I slept better when I had my own things. I also slept on 'his' side of the bed. I reclaimed the space I had before we had married. I also started a process of seeing what I wanted in a relationship. Through my inner work I was able to identify a repeated pattern I had in my two marriages. By claiming my dysfunctional behaviour I could also start the process of healing to bring a healthier relationship into my life.

What do you want in your life?

The Third Stepping-Stone: Letting Go

I wanted a job working with people to help them reclaim themselves. I had it that it must be in Scotland. I struggled with the place it had to be. This demand created so much emotional pain holding on. I finally let that go and asked God to tell me where I was to be. The result was the clear direction to do this work in the Czech Republic. I let go of my control and allowed myself to be sourced.

When Stacey moved from our house to her own so abruptly I was filled with pain and anger. After all, I wasn't prepared for it to happen then. My mind had another date. Also, I was letting go of a constant in my life which was my child, and facing the unknown alone. It was agonizing until I released my 'how it has to be' attitude and let her be free to be the adult she was striving to be.

I found that some friends I had before I started to do this work were now no longer comfortable with me as I had changed so much. As hard as I tried to get them to enter into the 'right' conversations or do courses I thought they 'needed' to be happy, they just wouldn't listen. I finally had to let go of my demand that my friends accept the changes in me as well as that they change to make me more comfortable. Some friends went away, others came in their place. We were all enriched by our experience.

What have you let go of lately in your journey of change? Did you find letting go painful?

_____

_____

_____

_____

The Fourth Stepping-Stone: Adjusting

One of the biggest adjustments I made was when I came to live in the Czech Republic. They were just free from communism. I had nothing when I arrived here. I literally left everything behind. I couldn't buy stamps or paper to write home, as I had no money. I slept in student housing with 17 sharing one bathtub and toilet. What I thought I needed to survive and what I actually needed were vastly different. I relaxed, adjusted and got used to having very little. Blessed were the days for an apple. What sustained me were the friends I made. We shared everything, especially tears and laughter.

I was used to being able to turn on the news, pick up a newspaper and find out about the world. Here there is a weekly English-language paper. I can read about the Czech Republic. I go for days, even weeks, without knowing what is going on in the world. I have adjusted to this, and now, when I go to the West, the news nearly assaults me.

When I lived in the United States I had credit cards and a cheque book. Of course, I had credit debt as well. For the past almost 10 years I have lived in a cash society. This was an incredible adjustment for me. No credit cards and no cheque books. We pay our bills at the bank. If we have money we think about spending it and when we do not have money, we just wait till the end of the month to get paid. It is truly another world and it feels so good not to be in debt.

When my husband Ken left us there was a big period of adjustment. I couldn't sleep in our bed for months. I slept on the couch. The silence was terrible. I missed having him there to talk to. I missed the fighting as it took up space in my day. I had to let go and, as a result, start to find myself.

What are some of the things you have had to adjust to lately? Has this adjustment helped you to decide what it is you really want?

_____

_____

_____

_____

The Fifth Stepping-Stone: Surrender

Sometimes it is extremely hard for me to see the gift in a situation, especially if I am suffering as a result. When I moved away from home, it was to find myself and be of service to others. The pain was because I was unable financially to travel home for seven years. I missed my daughter so much. Many things had changed. The gift I received was that in coming away from everything I knew, I found myself. I could, in turn, give this gift of authenticity to my family when I was with them again.

Every time I know best and think I must be the one to do all this work and, yes, save the world, I start feeling like I am pushing a very big rock up a mountain. The more I have to do this myself, the more I end up in a struggle. As a result, the journey is harder. When I notice I am doing this again, I let go and surrender. I open and allow the source to work through me. It is surprising how light the load gets.

My recent work has been in the area of my need for independence. I have always been one to do it myself. This stems from my trust issues. My biggest fear was I would become dependent on anyone for anything. At the root of this was that I would be let down. I now understand the cost of excluding people in my life because I couldn't trust them to be there for me. Surrendering this belief system and my 'have to' behaviour has allowed me to move into interdependence. Also, a great weight has been lifted from my shoulders.

What have you personally chosen to let go of or surrender lately? How has this surrender affected you?

_____

_____

_____

_____

The Sixth Stepping-Stone: In the Swim

I had been going through a very difficult period with regards to my work in this country. The Association became a heavy burden to carry. I took a period of time of silence to do some inner work. I realized it was my demand that it all look a certain way that was creating the problems. I surrendered my need to have the organization and all of a sudden it seemed to me that people were offering to help. Things began to change. I had let go and God/Life was helping me to be in the swim of life and love.

I haven't been in any close relationship in 17 years. I have played it safe by becoming a workaholic. My mind said this was justified as I was doing this for a very good cause, saving humanity. What I became painfully aware of was how much I had isolated myself, especially from men. I had buried my feminine, earthy, sexy side under the earth mother who took all to her bosom. I had not dated for 30 years. I was sure the 'rules' had changed. Recently, I have been corresponding with men over the Internet. It has been an excellent vehicle to get to know people. I have decided to turn this over to God. My intention is to have a loving supportive relationship. Once I gave up my fear about what would happen to me and chose to go with the flow, men have been entering my life who are beautifully sensitive and loving. I am enjoying being in the flow with this part of my life. My students have been sending energy for me to have a partner in my life. They are so pleased I have opened myself to this possibility. I have also realized that by opening myself to being intimate, it has given them the room to do the same.

The first time I went back to the United States to see my family, I had no idea how we would be with each other. It had been seven years. My daughter, Stacey, was expecting her second child very soon. My mother was being treated for terminal cancer and had been receiving energy from the Czech Republic from my students. When I was living in the States before I had such a strong control drama. My fear was I would just pick it up again. I prayed for direction. I asked God to guide me in being all I could experience myself to be in clarity and love. I released my fear. After a few days I realized I was seeing and experiencing my family from a different perspective. It was a blessing each day to spend time with them without many words. I experienced my daughter as a mother. I marvelled at her patience and understanding. I had no need to tell her how it should be done. I was the silent witness to her being.

I took my mother to the doctor and waited while she had a special x-ray. A nurse came into the waiting room and asked me to come in and talk to them. When I walked in the room my mom was telling the staff about Reiki. She explained that this love had been coming from a long distance to her for many months. She was especially happy when I would call her and tell her how many worked on her and how many of them were good-looking men. The staff were laughing. I asked what was going on. The doctor said, 'We are celebrating your mother's recovery from cancer. There is no longer a tumour. We had noticed it had been reducing in size, but today it has completely disappeared. She is saying it is because of Reiki. All we know is that it is a miracle. I do hope you will continue to send her this love. It has made the difference between life and death.' I never expected my mom to be a witness for Reiki. In her way, she was telling her story and touching others with possibility. What also occurred was a deeper healing for us. Our relationship had changed. I believe we were both willing to go with the flow and to see where it took us.

When was the last time you went with the flow of life? How did it feel to you? What realizations have you had as a result?

_____

_____

_____

_____

After answering the questions, take time to sit quietly and feel your body. Remember that revisiting areas of your life may also bring up emotions that you may not have expressed in a long time. Take the time to give yourself a self-treatment. By loving into yourself you set these emotions free and acknowledge the importance of each step you have taken.

Close your eyes and take a deep, cleansing breath. Feel your body. Are there areas that are tight or heavy? Are there places in you that need to be touched and loved into? Use your hands to touch these places. Give yourself Reiki to return these areas into harmony. If you have been initiated into Reiki two energy, use the power and emotional mental symbols to work deeply to return yourself to a state of inner harmony and peace.

Honour yourself and your journey thus far.

Without the Struggle, there are no Wings to Fly Free

There is a story about a family who found two cocoons. They watched one of the cocoons as it started to open and saw the pain the butterfly went through to get out of the cocoon and eventually to fly free. When the second one started to open the family thought they would help by splitting open the cocoon so the butterfly would not have to suffer. However, the wings of the butterfly never became strong and beautiful and it died. They were puzzled about this, and when they asked an entomologist why it had happened, he explained the pain was part of the process of birth and that it helped to make the butterfly healthy. In the birth process, a substance was released from the body of the butterfly that would strengthen not only the butterfly but also its wings so it could fly. In effect, their help actually killed the butterfly.

I started to think how we seem to want to have an easy time moving through life, and that the struggle is what we try to avoid at all costs. We often sabotage ourselves by not feeling the pressure or the pain. Avoidance thus becomes the main goal. In my own personal work on myself and with others I have realized how important feeling is. When we give ourselves permission to have the feeling, pain and pressure, we then can move through it and out to the other side. The butterfly represents the cocoon of transition from whatever life there was which usually was unsatisfactory, hence the need for change. A process occurs by nature, to experience the pain of moving into our authentic self. There is no way to short-circuit this process because the pain is needed to realize and own the transformation. If the process is brought about too fast (releasing the butterfly before experiencing the pain) the person then usually acts out of need rather than the desire to fly freely with their own wings.

I understand that for many of us undergoing the battle of life, it has been the passage from the cocoon we have been experiencing, and soon our wings will dry and we can fly free. The desire I have is that we also fly free in community. Oneness is the goal. I see us as a beautiful world community of butterflies emerging in our own state of struggle, the help is to wait and remind each other of our majesty and community, not to cut one free before the experience of our true selves. The journey is the joy, and the authentic expression of us. If the cocoon is split open before 'nature's process' is complete, we become paralysed by 'the light'. We will be unable to move, to express, to live, and we would die before expressing the beauty of our unique self, which is a precious gift.

I sat back and rested my eyes. It had been a long day with my students. In the process of their own story-telling, much pain was released and a deepening of personal commitment realized. I was feeling grateful for their work, our work in transforming old patterns of behaviour. The space in the castle seemed to take on a new brighter glow as we moved into our last night together. I wanted some direction or words that would touch their souls and acknowledge them for the steps they had taken…

You can say: choose in every moment to uphold the individual and uphold yourself. Acknowledge the gifts that each one brings to you and the world. Look for the light, not the darkness of people and situations. For in acknowledging light you breathe life into it and fan the flames of love. Take the time to be still and listen to the inner heartbeat of God. Practise 'being' rather than doing. The heart needs to experience beauty, give it beautiful moments. Soft touches, looking into the centre of a flower, hearing music that causes your soul to soar – all will benefit you. Treat yourself as your most precious lover. And, at the end of the day, be grateful for yet another day to make a difference in our world. These and more words like this are indeed inspiring. You know how to encourage others to feel and respond. You could write a beautiful letter and make a special ceremony of the gift. There are as many ways to touch into them as drops in the sea. Certainly, you can come up with something without my help, dear one. You surrender into the source time and time again. There is so much you can do, my darling, but wouldn't you much rather be? After all, isn't this the overall message in this book?

What is it you want to say from the bottom of your heart, dear one? Have you opened yourself fully to the wonders of being a human being and transforming? Sometimes words are not adequate to express the feelings that are so deeply spiritual that to even suggest a word would be to confine it and limit it in a way. Can it not be enough to simply look into the eyes of those people around you and without words convey the depth of your soul? Can your compassionate heart open so wide that the experience of being separate vanishes? What, then, is created is oneness, a knowing that is in the middle of all and is the way in and out of everything.

Stand before all people free of your masks, and without words invite them into you and an intimacy of the universal soul. Lose the place where you end and they begin. In that moment you will be also one with us. For we are one with you. No finer moment can be experienced…

To you who have read this book it is my intention that you have been touched with possibility. To also acknowledge your own personal journey you have taken into inner peace. To see how many steps you have walked, instead of the ones you need to take. For the mind will make the journey harder if you choose. To also know that all people in this beautiful world of ours are walking their own journey of discovery. Each one is different and unique to them. Some doorways will take more time to discover. Develop patience in the process of living. You will be supported in your process with the use of Reiki as it harmonizes both the cause and effect of the disharmony.

I believe we are standing at a new threshold. There is a doorway that is clearly in our view. It is one of community. For so long we have been self-defined. It is time to be in a bigger relationship and explore our place in the community of mankind. What will we find there as we open the door? We will find opportunities and stepping-stones. We will tell our communal stories, how we evolved what we as groups of people realized. We will make choices, evolve and transform and then what? Our future is as unlimited as we wish to create it. Shall we stand at the threshold together and embrace what lies ahead?

Come let us dance in the light of all that we are together!

PERSONAL
NOTES

Use the following pages to note down any extra thoughts or expand on any of your answers to the questions throughout this book.

_____

REIKI FOR THE SOUL

REIKI FOR THE SOUL

REIKI FOR THE SOUL

REIKI FOR THE SOUL

REIKI FOR THE SOUL